High 1
An Insig... ...ω insanity"

Ross Farrally

Printed by *Book Printing UK*

Copyright © 2020 Ross Farrally

All rights reserved. No part of this publication may be reproduced, distributed, or transmitted in any form or by any means, including photocopying, recording, or other electronic or mechanical methods, without the prior written permission of the publisher, except in the case of brief quotations in critical reviews and certain other noncommercial uses permitted by copyright law. For permission requests, write to the publisher at the address below.

Publisher: Independent Publishing Network.

Publication date: 01.04.2020

ISBN: 978-1-78972-688-6 (Paperback)

Front cover image by Ross Farrally
Book design by Ross Farrally

First printing edition 2020.

Printing: Book Printing UK

rosspublishing.net
www.facebook.com/highroydsbook
ross@aninsightintoinsanity.co.uk

In memory of my late father, Paul Farrally, who taught me that working for something is far more rewarding than being handed it.

1962 - 2011

DISCLAIMER

As this is my first venture into the world of literature, this entire journey has been a vast learning curve. It wasn't until I had all the interviews completed, that I came to realize the additional work that was required, such as gaining consent to publish the interviews and citing the resources that I have used.

By no means am I a historian, nor have I ever considered myself one. I have researched into High Royds, alongside the history of psychiatry, since the age of twelve as an out-of-school diversion.

That being said, I have tried with the upmost dedication to ensure that everything written in this book is factual and accurate to the best of my knowledge. I spent additional time re-learning the history of High Royds to ensure I present solid information to you, the reader, and I do sincerely apologize if anything you read may not be entirely correct. I have gone to great lengths to prevent this.

You also need to understand that these interviews are recollections of these individual's past. They will be stating their own opinions on the institution and many other subjects.

All of those who have been interviewed for this book have had their names changed to protect their identity, plus any additional individuals that they may have mentioned. I also took great care in ensuring that every story told here is suitable for the audience and for the nature of this book. I made it clear from the beginning of this journey that interviews that I deemed unacceptable wouldn't be included.

All interviewees gave their permission for their interview to be published after reading multiple amended versions of their discussion. They were supplied with the first draft in which they were free to make any suggestions before receiving a second draft with said changes made. Finally, they were presented with the finished product, displayed as it is laid out in this book. Only when they were entirely happy with the finished piece, they gave permission for publication.

I was criticized at the beginning of this mission as a select few individuals were under the impression that this book was a case study of the institution as a whole. This is entirely false. This book is merely a collection of interviews and in places of missing information; I have tried to piece it together. I am in no way educated enough to present a case study on the hospital, nor do I believe I am the right individual to do that.

Much like many other books in the market today, all of the factual information written here did not come solely from my mind. Besides my twelve years of knowledge on the subject, I had to piece fragments of information together by excessively researching old news articles, original documentation and medical journals. With that, I send my gratitude to the West Yorkshire National Archives for their preservation of the original High Royds documents. Any information that I have used from online sources, I have cited them at the close of this book.

To finalize, the views and opinions expressed in this book are those of the author and not necessarily reflect the official policy or position or any other agency, organization, employer or company.

***

ACKNOWLEDGEMENTS

I would like to start by thanking my mother. Without her, the institution would have never been known to me. From taking me to the old site at a young age, to providing me with information that filled in the blanks for many of these interviews. She has always been a successful woman, within her career and at motherhood. I am who I am today because of her.

I would also like to acknowledge my sister, Kimberley, who persisted that we enter the hospital through an open-door during demolition. Without that push into the unknown I would have never had the knowledge I do today of what happened behind those walls of High Royds. She has taught me many things, how to swim, how to ride a bike and now, taught me that you can reach great heights in our lives as long as you persevere.

None of this would have been possible either without my best friend, my partner, Katelyn. She encouraged me to write to the best of my ability and offered endless support whenever I required it. She willed me through the great lows of this journey, pressed me to continue this flight and provide a piece of work that I am honored to have taken on.

In addition, I would like to express the deepest appreciation to my interviewees. Without your stories and recollections this book would not have been possible. I and those who are reading will forever remember your bravery to come forward and tell your accounts of High Royds. The fear of being believed may continue to shadow you, but I hope this book presses you to continue expressing your story.

***

CONTENTS

Introduction	9
High Royds Hospital, Menston	12
Treatments	16
Beamsley Block	
Introduction	30
Yasmin Sherman	33
Ronald Flowers	39
Clyde Mallon	50
Clinton Lam	56
Harold Chapman	71
Ed Bolton	75
Emily Silva	78
Linn Baker	82
Norma French	86
Rhona Wade	90
Norwood House and Rigton	
Introduction	95
Cora Rowntree	99
Linton House	
Introduction	111
Gloria Rogers	113
Shannon Guise	125
Caitlin Eastcott	131
Rehabilitation Wards	
Introduction	134
Sandy Morgan	136
Summary	150
Laura Turner	152
References	158

INTRODUCTION

"During this early period (of the hospital) the patient discharge rate was only 30% of the annual admissions, while the mortality rate was as high as 15% per annum."

In 1888, the doors of the third West Riding Pauper Lunatic Asylum in Menston opened to help the overcrowding issues at the other county's asylums in Wakefield and Wadsley.

I have always said, "asylums were a great idea, but born during the wrong era." We built establishments for those who were deemed "imbeciles," "idiots," "dangerous lunatics" and the "mentally convalescent," with the idea to shut them off from the world and this is evident in how the institutions were planned and positioned, usually perched at the end of a stretched driveway that arched out of view, leaving those who stood at the end wondering what erected before them.

Institutions that cared for the mentally ill should not be forgotten. You could continuously argue many negative points about these hospitals, the conditions, the care and even the treatments that were presented to those who were suffering however, without these institutions; we may not have the understanding of mental health as we do today.

Many of us have personal connections to High Royds or other asylums around the country and many of these links present a biased opinion. Neglectful care of a loved one will instantaneously lead us to label these institutions as corrupt and immoral regardless of any stories presented to us that exhibit excellent care. This also works on the opposing side, where a relative or friend receives outstanding care from these institutions. Those who have only respectable things to say about asylums will silence the talk of neglect and mistreatment.

The goal of this book is not to end the stigma attached to these establishments, it is merely a gateway into asylum life, to understand what happened to those who hid in the asylum's shadow. It gives us a glimpse into how these individuals lived, how they coped and how they recovered with or without the aid of High Royds.

I also interviewed a couple of former nurses of the hospital who gave me an insightful look into how these institutes were run and their own thoughts on the stigma attached to asylums like High Royds.

You will read about the positive sides of the institution and how the dedicated staff helped aid the recovery of these struggling individuals, how they turned a bleak and misunderstood service into a place of refuge and safety for many inpatients.

The hospital also had its neglectful side, much like most asylums around the country, and I will present you with firsthand accounts of those who suffered abuse and mistreatment by the very same people they put their trust in.

The dates of these accounts play an important role in distinguishing when the hospital's care took an important turn, paying attention to individual needs and developing a care plan with the aim for discharge.

The procedures for asylum closure began to surface in the 1970s with High Royds managing to survive the first wave. Slowly, the services that the hospital offered began to relocate around the city, with patients being moved to other clinics such as Maple House at St. Mary's Hospital in Armley and The Mount on Hyde Terrace.

Many people believe that these societies closed down due to neglectful staff, abuse and poor conditions. You would be right in thinking that, but many of the country's asylums closed down as they were not fit for purpose, mainly due to the advancement in psychiatric care and High Royds was no different. The hospital became outdated, and many consultants stressed that more resources needed to be implemented into mental health services.

High Royds provided Menston and the surrounding villages with a refuge for those with mental illness for over a hundred and ten years. I hope you enjoy the accounts in this book that outline what life was like for those inside the institution and their families waiting on the outside.

***

HIGH ROYDS HOSPITAL, MENSTON

High Royds Hospital has an extensive history in which the majority of those from around the area will already be accustomed to. For those who are unaware, below is a brief history of Menston's psychiatric hospital.

In 1885, a three-hundred-acre estate to the south of the village of Menston was purchased for a sum of £18,000 by the West Riding Justices.

Architect J. Vickers Edwards was commissioned to design a layout for the hospital and later produced his broad arrow plan. Asylums around the country typically adopted one of the five main styles. They could categorize these as, Radial Plan, Corridor Plan, Pavilion Plan, Echelon Plan and Colony Plan.

The broad arrow plan consisted of the hospitals wards and services being spread out across the entirety of site. These services were then connected to a main corridor that ran the length of the main asylum.

High Royds Hospital was unique in the way they constructed it. There were only two examples of the broad arrow plan being built, with only one reaching full completion, this being High Royds. The second hospital to adopt this plan was Claybury Hospital but due to delays in construction, plans were changed midway through its erection.

Construction of the hospital lasted three years and by October 8th 1888, the asylum formally opened as the West Riding Pauper Lunatic Asylum.

They decorated the interior of the hospital to the highest standards possible. Italian marble floors and glazed tiles ornamented the main corridors of the establishment. Key rooms such as the ballroom were decorated with fine stained-glass windows and engraved wooden panels. According to a published report, the total sum of the original asylum amounted to £350,000, the equivalent to £150,000,000 today. This amount proved to be well spent as the hospital continued to stand tall and intact after 115 years of use.

One feature that was left out during the creation of High Royds was an on-site chapel. They included one in the original plans but this never came to completion. It was the only asylum in the country not to have its own chapel and remained this way until one was later provided. The original designs showcased a spectacular church, roughly one-hundred and sixty-feet in length, complete with steeple that towered to a height of around one-hundred-feet. They proposed it to fit the mold of a typical Victorian church with plans showing gothic, hood style arches for doorways and windows. In November 1967, 79 years after the opening of the asylum, they finally built a chapel on-site. This place of worship merely lasted thirteen years before being demolished by a fire in 1980. Three years later and the final chapel of High Royds were built, positioned behind and to the left of the administration building.

During its creation, the hospital constructed a short railway to ferry building supplies to the site. After the asylum was built, its use continued sparingly until its final closure in 1951. Prior to its closure, it was commonly used to carry supplies such as flour and mostly coal for fuel in the hospital's boilers.

They designed the hospital to be an enclosed community, offering many onsite services such as its own library, surgery, dispensary, butchery, bakery and a large estate devoted to agriculture and market gardening.

High Royds offered many other services but the majority of these, including those that I have listed, seized its services as the years progressed. I believe this may have been due to introduction of antipsychotics, which allowed patients to finally leave the confines of the asylum but I am unable to confirm if this was the sole reason.

The general wards in the hospital were designed to accommodate a large number of patients in one room. They did this with no partitions between patient bedsides to allow for simplified observations from the nursing staff.

They referred to this method of arrangement as the Nightingale. Each ward was also accompanied by its own sanitary services and a small number of seclusion rooms.

They divided the original patients of the hospital into two groups, private patients who could afford to pay for their treatment and those who were referred by the Poor Law Unions, either from their resident workhouses or as direct admissions. Private patients were allowed to wear their own clothes and were tended to in private suites rather than the universal Nightingale wards.

Work, amusements and exercise were a few of the significant features of the asylum regime with the intention of distracting the patient's mind and attention from the causes of their illness. Patients who did not require close supervision were active in a range of outdoor employments, such as tending to the garden and working on the asylum's farm. Those who could not work outside were introduced to indoor occupations. These included services such as the tailor's shop and boot makers. They invited those who were capable to play on the sports teams based out of the hospital. One of these being the cricket team that had its own field to the east of the hospital. The climax of the asylum week was the Friday night dance in the ballroom, one of the few occasions for male and female patients to mix.

By 1898, High Royds underwent an expansion in order to increase its capacity. On its original completion, High Royds had the facilities to house approximately 1400 patients but ten years later, after the addition of the extra pavilions, the patient count reached 1526. In 1902, a further block for male chronic patients was constructed to add an extra 120 beds.

Patients who were detained during the earlier days of the asylum may have found themselves living out their remaining days there. Lives that were lost at the asylum were buried in unmarked graves throughout the local graveyards. It wasn't until 1906 that the hospital acquired its own cemetery alongside the railway, in which 2858 patients remain buried today. Those buried at the cemetery, known as Buckle Lane, were also allocated unmarked graves but today, those running the chapel have gone to great lengths in placing names to these lost souls, ensuring they are remembered by following generations.

Attitudes towards mental illness radically changed in the 1920s and the hospital continued the drive, dropping its original name in favor of the West Riding Mental Hospital.

In 1949, the name was altered once more, replacing the 'West Riding' with Menston, thus becoming Menston Mental Hospital.

As the psychiatric world continued to evolve, the hospital once again reformed and in 1952, became known as simply, Menston Hospital. It was around this time that the world was introduced to the first antipsychotic, the same drug that would begin a revolution, attempting to bring an end to the asylum regime. It was these medications that pressed the medical world to question the continued existence of these institutions.

The hospitals final change came in 1964, altering its title to High Royds Hospital. This also encouraged the hospital to expel ward numbers in favor of names taken from villages in the Yorkshire Dales. For example, renamed the wards that were situated in the admissions block to Denton, Clifton, Langbar and Beamsley.

The adaption to community care was discussed in the 1960s, with closure plans outlined for numerous asylums around the country however, due to lack of finance and political will, these plans never came to fruition and the hospitals remained in operation.

I believe it was the early 1980s when High Royds was marked for closure, with many services being moved off site and into other psychiatric facilities throughout the city.

By 2003, the last of the services were terminated and the hospital closed its doors on psychiatric health care, bringing to an end 115 years of inpatient care.

***

TREATMENTS

The advancement in treatments for the mentally ill have progressed significantly since the days of bloodletting and trephination but that is not to say that the treatments that followed were any less cruel and degrading than those of its ancestors.

High Royds was at the forefront of modern psychiatric care, replacing sedation and locked wards with occupational therapy and freedom. Even with this enhanced asylum model, abuse was still present within the walls of the hospital, despite the efforts of many devoted staff.

I have chosen not to cover many of the well-known treatments such as physical restraints and trephination; the practice of drilling holes into patient's skull to create exits for spirits. This is since they are well known amongst the general population or were carried out during the Neolithic period.

I cannot be certain that all the following treatments were used at High Royds but I can confirm that they were carried out in similar institutions around the county.

I. BLOODLETTING AND PURGING

Bloodletting dates back to the times of the Mayans, Aztecs, Egyptians and Mesopotamians. This practice is known to be one of the oldest medical treatments and was used to cure a person of illnesses such as leprosy, acne, plague, inflammation, stroke, pneumonia, herpes and many other ailments.

The aim of Bloodletting was to remove the patient's illness through the flow of their blood. Practitioners would create a small cut on a particular part of the patient based on their sickness. A gash in the elbow was marketed to cure a strained back or arm, while a small incision in the temple was said treat a headache or non-violent insanity.

The practice continued to be popular in the 19th century, where leaches would be used to drain the patient's blood. As the century progressed, medical practitioners questioned the practice of bloodletting after realizing that it killed more people than it cured.

Despite the decline of it use, during the early 20th century, The Principles and Practice of Medicine textbook, dated 1923, outlined that Bloodletting had four popular processes:

- Leaches.
- Arteriotomy - puncturing the arteries in the temples.
- Phlebotomy - a large external vein would be cut to draw blood.
- Scarification - possibly the most punishing of the methods, which involved using countless sets of tools to puncture the shallow blood vessels.

The use of Bloodletting has now seen a significance decrease but continues to be used for a small number of conditions and surgical procedures in today's medicine.

II. THE GYRATING CHAIR

The Gyrating Chair was a widespread tool introduced in the mid-1700s by Dr. Boerhaave, with its popularity peaking in both Europe and the United States.

Original artwork of the device illustrates a patient strapped into a sitting position within an upright wooden container. The "chair" is positioned above the ground, secured to a pole that connects to both the floor and ceiling. To the patient's left, perched upon a raised platform, stands the individual in charge of the procedure. A rod connects to the patient's pole which allows for the chair to be spun by whoever is on the controlling end.

Spinning at speeds of 100rmp (rotations per minute), this machine was intended to shake up the blood and tissues of the brain to create a calm state of mind and increase blood supply to the brain.

In a majority of the cases, the patient would be rendered unconscious and showed no signs of improvement, concluding the procedure to be unsuccessful.

It is unknown how long this device was in operation for but based on the time period it was in commission, it may have been used in asylums such as Bethlem Royal Hospital, Manchester's Royal Lunatic Asylum, St Luke's Hospital for Lunatics and many others that were open during the mid-1700s.

I. HYDROTHERAPY

Hydrotherapy is commonly referred to as cold water therapy however; hydrotherapy consists of a variety of water temperatures. Most of us are under the impression that patients were doused in cold water, usually to correct bad behavior. This is correct however; warm water was also used in therapeutic ways to aid one's recovery.

The method was introduced into asylum life at the beginning of the 20th century and was deemed a popular method for treating those suffering from a mental illness.

The use of water to aid recovery was seen as affective due to the endless possibilities of methods that could be created. The water could be cooled or heated and applied to the patients in a variety of ways to produce an array of reactions.

It was deemed affective due to its ability to take effect quickly.

Hydrotherapy could be accomplished in many ways using a variety of aids such as baths, sheets or sprays.

Patients who were diagnosed as insomniacs would have found themselves submerged in bathtubs of hot water. These bathing periods would last for hours, overnight or continuous days. To ensure this type of treatment was most effective, they would be held in quiet, isolated areas with little light and decreased audio stimulation, thus allowing the patient to relax and possibly even fall asleep. Temperatures for these baths would typically range from 33-36 degrees Celsius.

These bathtubs were no different than the common household ones, except with the addition of a running metal road that ran the perimeter of the tub, just underneath the rim. Attached to this, draped across the whole of the tub, was a large white canvas. This covered the entirety of the bath, exposing only the head which allowed the patient to be fed by local nurses. I am unsure whether they were cocooned in this way to prevent the heat from escaping; allowing for a longer bathing period or it was done as physical restraint. The design of the baths allowed the staff to add additional amounts of hot water while draining the colder water, thus allowing prolonged bathing periods. Immersed to their chin, patients' heads would rest on a rubber pillow.

Wraps attempted to follow the same method as continuous baths and consisted of submerging a large sheet in water, either cold or warm, and encasing the patient for multiple hours.

Sprays were delivered much like showers, dowsing patients in a mixture of water temperatures. Cold water was used to treat those diagnosed with manic-depressive psychoses as the low temperature was known to reduce the blood flow to the brain, decreasing the individual's mental and physical activity. Cold water therapy used temperatures as low as four degrees Celsius.

I. INSULIN COMA THERAPY

Insulin Shock Therapy, or as it is most commonly known, Insulin Coma Therapy (ICT), was a practice that induced comas in mainly schizophrenic patients through the use of insulin. It was introduced into the psychiatric world in 1927 by Austrian-American psychiatrist Manfred Sakel and used extensively between 1940-1950.

When introduced into inpatient psychiatric care, ICT was delivered by professionally trained staff within a specialist unit. Those who were diagnosed as schizophrenic were prime candidates for this treatment under the basis of having a good prognosis and the physical strength to withstand the grueling treatment.

There were no set guidelines for this treatment, with many hospitals and psychiatrists developing their own protocols. Naturally, individuals could find themselves being administered injections six days a week for two months.

Insulin is used in the treatment of people with type one diabetes who produce little or no insulin. It may also be used in the treatment of type two diabetes. Insulin is a hormone that is produced by the pancreas and allows your body to use sugar from carbohydrates in the food that you eat for energy or to store sugar for future use. Insulin helps keeps your blood sugar level from getting too high or too low. After you eat food and your blood sugar level rises, cells in your pancreas are signaled to release insulin into your bloodstream. Insulin then attaches to and signals cells to absorb sugar from the bloodstream. If too much insulin is administered, the blood sugar levels can decrease to a dangerous level.

This was the strategy when performing ICT. The aim was to inject the patient with near fatal doses of insulin to the extent where a hypoglycemic coma was produced.

In order to know the exact amount of insulin needed to produce a coma, patients were injected daily with each one being an increased amount from the last. This continued until the patients were being administered between 100 and 150 units at a time. At this point, they would slip into their insulin coma. On occasions, it was known that up to 450 units of insulin could be used. When the exact number of units was known, the dose was leveled out and patients would be subjected to around sixty individual comas, or less if the psychiatrist thought that maximum benefit had been achieved. Before the therapy was stopped entirely, the dose of insulin prescribed was reduced dramatically.

With such high levels of insulin being given to the patient, they would exhibit a variety of symptoms including, but not limited to, decreased blood sugar, flushing, salivation, drowsiness and restlessness. If the dose was high enough, a coma would follow. Each coma would last for up to an hour and be concluded by intravenous glucose or via a feeding tube threaded through the nose and into the stomach. It was common for seizures to sometimes occur before or during the coma and many would show signs of physical frustration and be unable to keep still, tossing and twitching.

When these carefully selected individuals were not unconscious, they were cared for very carefully by the units dedicated staff and were subject to special treatment with outdoor walks, games and competitions.

The most severe risks of insulin coma therapy were death and brain impairment, resulting from either an irreparable or extended coma. A study at the time claimed that many of the cases of brain impairment were actually therapeutic improvement because the patient's level of resentment and aggression rapidly decreased.

I. METRAZOL THERAPY

Coma therapy continued to be a popular treatment option in the early 20th century, with Metrazol therapy entering the market.

The Hungarian physician, Ladislaus von Meduna, conducted clinical experiments with Metrazol in 1933 and shortly after, it was introduced into the asylums. He had attempted to use many other drugs prior to Metrazol such as Strychnine, Thebain and Pilocarpin. However, it was Metrazol that gave the most promising results.

The drug was given via intramuscular injection and produced epileptic convulsions. Meduna produced an argument that those suffering from both epilepsy and schizophrenia could possibly be cured of the latter based on his observations of fellow patients. Those who he witnessed having epileptic seizures would experience a remission of their symptoms of schizophrenia.

Patients would most commonly be stationed in bed during this therapy. Prior to the therapy beginning, the patients would be fitted with a mouth guard to prevent themselves from biting down on their tongue. After the dose of Metrazol was given, patients would begin to seize.

After 110 experiments, Meduna reported a discharge rate of 50%, with many showing extraordinary improvements. It is to note that 42% of individuals undergoing this treatment suffered from fractured spines due to the severity of their convulsions.

Metrazol therapy only lasted merely six years as towards the early 1940s, the therapy was replaced by Electroconvulsive Therapy. Studies concluded that

Metrazol therapy was far less effective than Insulin therapy in the treatment of schizophrenia.

I. LOBOTOMY

The lobotomy, alongside ECT, is one of the most commonly known psychiatric treatments amongst today's population. The history of this treatment is profound as well as time consuming so I will aim to cover only significant areas.

The earlier methods of the lobotomy, or as it was known originally, a leucotomy, involved cutting into the patient's skull and injecting ethanol into the brain to terminate the fibers that connected the frontal lobe to other parts of the brain. This was performed by the Portuguese neurologist Antonio Egas Moniz in 1935 which he later, in 1949, received the Nobel Prize in medicine.

Our prefrontal cortex is the control panel for our personality and contributes to an extensive variety of purposes such as, but not limited to, focusing one's attention, impulse control, future planning and coordinating.

By extinguishing fibers in this part of the brain, it rendered the patients dull and emotionless, thus, "cured" from their mental illness.

One year later, in 1936, The American physician, Walter Freeman, alongside his friend and colleague, the neurosurgeon James Watts, adapted Moniz's practice to create the "Freeman-Watts technique." This technique was the prefrontal lobotomy, shorted to lobotomy by Freeman himself.

Freeman's technique followed that of Antonio's, so an operating theatre was still required alongside trained neurosurgeons. Freeman believed that this would not be possible to perform in asylums due to the lack of operating rooms, surgeons, anesthesia and the limited budgets.

Freeman had the idea to create a more efficient way to perform a lobotomy, a way that allowed psychiatrists to carry out the procedure rather than neurosurgeons, making it available in institutions around the world. This led Freeman to create the ten-minute transorbital lobotomy, most commonly referred to as the 'ice-pick' lobotomy which he first performed in January 1946.

The NPR (National Public Radio) article, described the procedure as follows:

"As those who watched the procedure described it, a patient would be rendered unconscious by electroshock. Freeman would then take a sharp ice pick-like instrument, insert it above the patient's eyeball through the orbit of the eye, into the frontal lobes of the brain, moving the instrument back and forth. Then he would do the same thing on the other side of the face."

Freeman's new procedure had come at a time when asylums were becoming severely overcrowded and treatments for the mentally ill were desperate. This allowed his icepick lobotomy to become wildly popular.

In 1967, after over 4000 lobotomies, Freeman carried out his last procedure before being expelled from operating. His embargo came after a third lobotomy on one of his longtime patients who developed a brain hemorrhage and passed away.

By the mid-1950s, the procedure began to subside as scientists developed antipsychotics and antidepressant medications that were much more effective in treating these ill individuals.

I.   ELECTROCONVULSIVE THERAPY

Electroconvulsive Therapy, or ECT, is one of the most stigmatized mental health treatments in the history of psychiatric therapies.

The idea was born from the Italian psychiatrist Ugo Cerletti in 1938. Ugo's development of the treatment came after being inspired by a call to a slaughterhouse located in Rome. This abattoir had a method of enervating pigs with electric shocks, rendering them lifeless before slaughtering them.

In 1939, Professor Lucien Golla, a Neurologist and Mental Pathologist, was offered the Medical Director role at the newly opened Burden Neurological Institute in Bristol. After his appointment, Golla acquired the services of Dr Walter Grey, a pioneering neurophysiologist who established the first commercially viable electric shock machine in the United Kingdom. Throughout the 1970s, Golla and Grey continued to study and practise ECT at Golla's Burden Neurological institute.

The placement of the electrodes evolved throughout the years of its use. Originally, the conductors were positioned bilaterally, one on either side of the temple however, this caused memory disturbances and confusion. Due to this, two modified versions of the therapy came to light. The first was the change of positioning for the electrodes. They were now placed unilaterally, meaning they were placed on one side of the patient's head. This reduced the severity of the side effects, most noticeably the patient's orientation which resolved more rapidly. The second alteration changed the delivery of the shock. Previously, the current passed simultaneously but now, a brief pulse of electricity was used. However, it took many years for brief-pulse equipment to be implemented.

The first use of electroconvulsive therapy is referred to as the "unmodified" form. This was carried out without anaesthetic or muscle relaxants. Many psychiatrists argued that the use of anaesthetic was impractical as the initial shock from the machine would render the patient unconscious.

By the late 1940s/early 50s, the practice was modified once more by introducing two drugs to the therapy.

Before muscle relaxants were introduced into the practice, Curare, a South American muscle-paralyzing poison, was experimented with. Prior to use of Curare, the electrical currents passing through the patients would cause them to convulse, leaving the individuals with fractures and dislocations.

This muscle-paralyzing drug acted as the original muscle relaxant. Suxamethonium was introduced in 1951, replacing the use of Curare, thus making the practice safer which paved the way to a more widespread use of "modified" ECT. Soon after, a short-acting anaesthetic was paired with the muscle relaxant in order to spare patients the frightening sensation of suffocation that can be experienced with the drug.

The steady development of antidepressant uses, along with adverse portrayals of ECT in the media, led to a deterioration of its use during the 1950s to the 1970s.

A variation of the treatment remains in use today and is only issued as a last resort when all other treatment options have been exhausted. Before the treatment begins, patients are subject to a variety of physical and mental health checks to ensure that there are no medical conditions that would prevent them from receiving the therapy. There are many other protocols to follow and the one just written is one of many.

II. MEDICATIONS

Following the Second World War, the breakthrough in the development of effective psychiatric drugs allowed inhabitants of the asylums to live "normal" lives outside of the hospitals shadow. Due to the nature of their history, I will only be covering the fragments I believe are beneficial for the book.

I. ANTIHISTAMINES AND PROMETHAZINE

The first antipsychotics were born from the invention of antihistamines in the 1940s and 50s. These original antihistamines often produced episodes of sleepiness and sedation. Today's modern antihistamines are designed to ensure they don't reach the brain and are therefore less sedative. The research around developing antihistamines progressed into the introduction of promethazine, a drug that produced sedative side effects and was prescribed as a calming agent prior to a patient's surgery. It was this tranquilising effect that allowed pharmacologists and psychiatrists to consider using it to settle those suffering the positive symptoms in schizophrenia. These indications include hallucinations, delusions and movement disorders. These medications weren't immediately made available to the asylum population, they were vigorously tested on rats and healthy individuals and went through periods of modification until they were deemed suitable for the establishments.

II. LITHIUM

In 1948, an Australian psychiatrist by the name of John Cade made the discovery that lithium could aid as an effective treatment for manic depression, known today as bipolar disorder. One year later, after extensive research and subpar trials, he published the first paper on the use of lithium in the treatment of acute mania.

Lithium treatment continued to evolve and High Royds Hospital was at the front of this revolution. Dr Roy Hullin, a former Senior Lecturer at the University of Leeds, was at the forefront of this drive, using lithium to prevent recurrent events of depression and mania. Studies by Hullin and his team concluded that the use of lithium removed the patient's manic symptoms in a way more beneficial to the patient. Indicators such as restlessness and hyperactivity would dissolve without the need for drugs that induced states of sedation.

As reported by the University of Leeds, Dr Roy Hullin passed away on the 6th May 2012. The leeds.ac.uk website lists many of Hullin's accomplishments. Below, is an extract from the website.

"He also held a Welcome Fellowship between 1972 and 1977 and was appointed to two honorary directorships at High Royds Hospital, where he conducted much of his research: Honorary Director of the Regional Metabolic Research Unit in 1962 and Honorary Deputy Director of the Pathology Laboratories at High Royds in 1976. He retired from the University in 1989, although he was reappointed as an Associate Lecturer in Chemical Pathology until 1991".

III. THE FIRST ANTIPSYCHOTICS

Chlorpromazine, the first anti-psychotic drug, was first manufactured in 1950 and became commonly available for medical use by the mid-1950s. It was developed off the back of promethazine, with many individuals contributing to its eventual birth. In the beginning, much like promethazine, it was prescribed to calm patients prior to surgery but shortly after; psychiatrists took note of its calming effect and began issuing it to their patients.

This drug became the first stake in the heart of the asylum system, allowing those who were confined to these institutions a chance to leave the Victorian establishments. This also paved the way for local governments to cut costs and close these hospitals however; the community care that was promised to these individuals was not fulfilled, permitting the asylums to continue its operation for decades to come. This medication was categorised as first-generation antipsychotics, meaning further development of this drug allowed a wave of improved antipsychotics to enter the psychiatric world.

The second-generation of antipsychotics to enter the market were, but not limited to, clozapine, olanzapine and risperidone. Unlike the first wave, these second-generation drugs had fewer effects on the patient's motor movement.

The third-generation brought further improvement, one of these being the ability to remove the sedation effect.

It is considered that no antipsychotic has been shown to be knowingly more effective than chlorpromazine in treating schizophrenia with the notable exception of clozapine.

One common medication found throughout the interviews in this book is the Modecate injection. The medicines.org.uk website outlines the use of this medication for:

"The treatment and maintenance of schizophrenic patients and those with paranoid psychoses.

While Modecate injection has been shown to be effective in acute states, it is particularly useful in the maintenance treatment of chronic patients who are unreliable at taking their oral medication, and also of those who do not absorb their oral phenothiazine adequately."

Many of the patients I came across had come into contact with this drug either directly or indirectly.

***

PART ONE

BEAMLSEY BLOCK

An eighty-meter-long dwelling stood to the left of the administration block and within its walls were four wards: Denton, Clifton, Langbar (which was the Intensive Care Unit) and Beamsley (the Occupational Therapy ward). According to an official script from the BBC TV series Bodies, which was filmed there in 2005, this was known as the Beamsley Block.

If you were to look at the premises front on, you would have seen Denton ward on the top floor, west side, with Langbar below and Clifton, also on the top floor, but to the east, with Beamsley underneath. The outside resembled more of a Victorian school rather than an asylum, with its rows of glass windows which sat neatly above blue plates of plastic. In terms of shape, the building was erected in a simple rectangle which connected to the rest of the hospital by one of the infamous double aspect corridors.

Décor was simple once inside and was consistent throughout the whole block. Light blue walls ran down either sides of the fairly-wide corridors with dark blue carpeting placed in the entrance way. As you made your way further into the establishment, the carpet came to a halt and an orangey-salmon lino took its place, curving a few centimetres up the adjoining walls. Corridors found themselves partitioned by fire doors, coloured similar to the earlier carpet. White wooden frames surrounded each door which also encased Georgian frosted wired glass, thus not allowing wandering eyes to peer between sections. Rooms that broke off from the corridor were also painted in light, refreshing colours such as yellow, orange, purple and blue. The waiting areas were filled with sub-standard chairs littered with magazines and showcased a dark orange carpet to match the lighter shade on the walls. A reception area could be found alongside the waiting room which was just as equally small.

To give you a quick breakdown of each ward, Langbar was labelled as an Intensive Care Unit (ICU). An ICU in a general hospital would be used to monitor very ill patients who have either had a serious accident, serious short-term condition or have just had major surgery. As much as this may have been required at High Royds, I believe that Langbar was actually a PICU (Psychiatric Intensive Care Unit). These units provided mental health care and treatment for people who were labelled as an absconding risk, suicidal or exhibited challenging behaviour and required a secure environment beyond that which could normally be provided on an open psychiatric ward. Denton and Clifton were both standard wards and Beamsley was a dedicated Occupational Therapy (O.T) ward. Beamsley would have been used by patients from across the entire hospital and allowed them to participate in activities such as painting, pottery class and many other "healing" projects.

By viewing my own photographs of the wards, there looked to be confinement cells, also known as isolation/monitoring rooms. They were empty, isolated and only held a single bed, built maybe half-a-foot off the ground. These simple beds were merely concrete blocks painted to match the walls which were a washed-out orange. Curved mirrors, that sat flush against the corners of the ceiling, were implemented to allow an unrestricted view of the cell. This meant that patients, who found themselves locked away, couldn't escape the watchful eyes of the orderlies standing on the other side of the door. These mirrors were most importantly used for staff safety so approaching staff members could pin-point the patient's exact location within the room. There were two doors to each isolation room and one may wonder why this was. Having two doors allowed an extra entrance for staff members to enter when it came to restraints. Staff members could enter through both doors at the same time or use one door as a form of distraction. Only one of the doors had a wired glass window, this was done so the patient couldn't see if anyone was behind the second door.

During the occasional recreation time, patients could enjoy a game of basketball on the small court to the rear of the building. The court was surrounded by the exterior walls of the Beamsley Block on one side and roughly an eight-foot green fence on the adjacent side. Small two-person benches were also implemented at the edge of the playing area to allow non-playing patients to observe.

***

YASMIN SHERMAN

1949

Yasmin reeled off memories from her time at High Royds, rather than run me through a chronological account like most of my other interviewees. None the less, Yasmin's stories gave me as much insight into High Royds as the others.

At nineteen, Yasmin began training as a children's nurse at Bradford Children's Hospital but due to ill-health, her time there was only short - three months to be exact, before moving on to High Royds Hospital or, as it was called at the time, Menston Hospital.

Prior to her move to the asylum, she worked in a greengrocer's shop in Guiseley, which was run by one of her friend's father from her time at Bradford Children's Hospital. Her friend's mother, who was working at High Royds at the time, encouraged Yasmin to reconsider her career as a nurse and work alongside her. Yasmin began her placement at High Royds in 1949, only spending a year at the institution before deciding that psychiatric nursing was not for her.

Drawing on her experience at High Royds, she explained that all new nurses to the institution were placed on the admissions ward, which I believe were Denton and Clifton, and only consisted of around twenty beds with both men and women segregated.

During her time there, Yasmin was housed in a bedsit, along with other nurses on the same corridor in the asylum, with the hospital taking a deduction from her wage to cover the cost of her room. She remembers the staff being treated well and always having good cooked food. Her social life was spent with her colleagues, some evenings enjoying the social life at the

Hare and Hound pub just to the south-east of the hospital on Bradford Road and having supper at Harry Ramsden's fish and chip restaurant just across from the hospital. On her off-duty weekends, she enjoyed shopping and cinema visits to Leeds and Bradford or visiting home to her family.

Her uniform consisted of a white striped dress with matching butterfly, black stockings and black shoes. She also noted that nurses would wear different coloured arm bands, each representing a level of nursing. Nurses today, in the NHS, have different colours to represent their role, from staff nurses to matrons however, in some A&E departments; they also have stickers that they place across the cuff of their uniform which display their role for the shift.

After a brief introductory chat in our interview, Yasmin began sieving through memories of her time spent in the hospital.

She first spoke about the admission ward she was housed on, Clifton. Yasmin described the ward as having two padded-cells in addition to about ten or twelve beds in the main ward. She remembers one patient, a young girl who had just passed her school exams, that came into High Royds due to a breakdown, probably caused by the stress induced during her examinations. She was described as having insisted on taking off all of her clothes which prompted the staff to house her in one of the confinement cells for a short amount of time. I believe that there was something more to this; maybe she displayed some violent or unpleasant behaviour to the staff or other patients. The girl was later given ECT and gradually got better according to Yasmin which prompted her discharge however, she was shortly brought back.

During Yasmin's era, ECT was carried out much differently to how it was when it was first introduced. With this in mind, I will explain the procedures for this therapy as it were in 1949.

In the 1950s, a patient hospitalized for depression stood an excellent chance of receiving ECT, and an even better chance of benefiting from it.

One distressing aspect of this young girl's stay at High Royds is that her aunt was also a patient in the hospital and Yasmin remembers that when she saw her niece walk past her bed she hid herself under the bedclothes, apparently feeling a sense of guilt that the taint of mania had manifested itself in one so young as her niece. Yasmin noted that the niece, when her condition was severe, referred to herself as royalty, which meant the staff members who passed by her bed had to bow.

Yasmin also talked about another patient whom she described as having "full moon disorder," a condition which supposedly, when the moon is shown to be full, affects an individual's mood. This has not been scientifically proven as scientists have come up empty-handed when investigating the correlation between full moons and behavioural changes.

Arnold Lieber, a psychiatrist who wrote the book "How the Moon Affects You", argued, rather unscientifically, that the moon has an effect on the human body (which is 65% percent water) that is similar to its pull on the ocean's tides.

In this case, Yasmin explained that the patient's eyes would change, that they looked "evil looking" and it would take three staff members to carry her off into one of the seclusion cells. She would claw at the faces of the staff and they would have to take extra measures when entering her room. Delivering a meal to her in her room had to be attended by three members of staff - one to take it in and two to watch for any threatening movements. During one shift, Yasmin remembered that the ward was short staffed due to sickness so she had to take the patient's meal in on her own. The woman was found to be lying in her bed, unstirred. Yasmin gently pushed the door open but was met by an ominous gaze from the patient. Sensing an imminent attack, Yasmin rushed in, dropping the tray of food on the women's bedside table before turning her back and heading for the exit. Just as she locked the door behind her, she heard the tray of food crash against door.

On one of her morning shifts, Yasmin, who was still in training, went to make up one of the patient's beds when she was attacked by the occupant, pulling at her hair, scratching and eventually pulling off Yasmin's cap. She explained that she subsequently learned patients saw their beds as places of safety so you had to be alert when approaching their personal space.

Yasmin spoke about the different types of treatments available at High Royds, one being insulin treatment and the second, Electroconvulsive Therapy.

She didn't speak much about the insulin treatment, only noting that patients given too much of the drugs were sent into convulsions.

The second treatment Yasmin spoke about was ECT. She began by explaining that a select number of patients were chosen and taken over to the unit where it was carried out. The patients who were selected were made to wait in the room adjacent to the treatment room and were called through one at a time. While the patient was being positioned on the table, Yasmin explained that there would be two nurses either side in order to restrain the patients, preventing them from exiting the table during their convulsions. This makes me believe that the treatment that Yasmin saw and participated in was the unmodified version of ECT.

While the patient was awake during the procedure, they were known to scream and convulse. Yasmin explained that these screams weren't cries caused by pain, they occurred as the air was being "ripped out of their body" which manifested itself as a scream. She explained that once the machine had been turned on, the current would render them unconscious. Once the patient's session had ceased, they had no recollection of what had happened as it gave them amnesia - memory issues caused by a shock to the brain. Yasmin remembered an improvement from the patients who underwent ECT and recalled that the mania they sometimes demonstrated had greatly lessened.

Yasmin then spoke about the "big house," noting that it contained one of the hospital's "most violent wards" which housed roughly ninety patients, with most of them being sedated. Yasmin referred to the ward as the "90s ward" which is probably due to the amount of beds it housed.

I looked into the wards of High Royds in more detail and couldn't find anything that would resemble a ward big enough for this number of patients. The only one that would come close would be the block that housed the Rigton and Lindley wards. The block was referred to as the chronic block which could have housed patients suffering from Schizoaffective Disorder which is a chronic mental health condition characterized primarily by symptoms of schizophrenia, such as hallucinations or delusions, and symptoms of a mood disorder, such as mania and depression.

The patients of High Royds were terrified of the "big house" Yasmin said, as it meant that they would then be long-stay patients at the hospital with very little chance of release back into the world. She remembered one girl who was petrified and had to be escorted into a van and lied to regarding their expected destination. She was apparently told she was going for a drive through Bradford. However, the van was driven around the grounds then toward the back door of the unit and the girl was taken in there. Another girl Yasmin remembered had turned catatonic when the "big house" was mentioned but the staff had to use their best efforts to move her there, one way or another.

Yasmin also spoke about the Friday night dances that took place in the ballroom of High Royds.

The ballroom stood just behind the administration building and was at the centre of the main corridor that ran across the entire site. It measured roughly 150 feet by 60 feet. The ceiling of the hall was decorated in mosaic tiles and met with a striking yellow paint. The Moroccan style wallpaper wrapped around the halls that met with a short running or green tiles. The floor was wooden, original and dark in colour, eventually weathered away by the footfalls of the Friday night balls.

Once a week, on a Friday evening, the women and men of High Royds would meet in the ballroom to dance. Yasmin explained that if a male patient asked you to dance then you had to accept. She remembered two male patients fighting amongst each other over who would dance with her but the situation was quickly resolved when one of the attendants escorted both men back to their dormitories.

Yasmin explained that as part of their daily routine the fitter male patients would tend to the gardens surrounding the hospital while the women did domestic duties such as working in the onsite laundry.

Yasmin left a year after she began. She never resumed her nursing career, turning instead towards the world of academe, teaching and writing. She is now known to be a historian of two books on women's history during the 19th century.

***

RONALD FLOWERS

1961

Heather's father, Ronald Flowers, was originally diagnosed to have suffered a nervous breakdown; however, it was later corrected to be PTSD. Ronald's story is something that many discharged soldiers still suffer with today. The battlefield can be a life altering place and Ronald is a prime example of that.

Heather began by speaking about her father. She labelled him as a "master tailor," someone who "loved dancing" and "loved his family."

Ronald had served in the army at the young age of fifteen. Heather said that you had to be sixteen to serve in the force but somehow, her father had managed to enrol a year early.

Ronald was a member of the 153rd Infantry Brigade of the 5th Battalion of the Black Watch. He was part of the operation, codenamed Operation Overlord, which was the battle of Normandy in 1944.

For work after the force, Ronald worked on and off at a tailor based in Kirkstall. The business was known locally as "John Collier's" and he worked there from the age of 31 until his retirement at sixty. During his spare time, Heather also said that her father made suits at home privately.

She was just seven years old when her father was admitted to Menston. The events that led him to his stay in High Royds began one lunch time at home. Heather mentioned that there was a gas leak which had caused her father to go "berserk" with a "poker" (the object that was used to stoke the older fireplaces.) During his moment of rage, Ronald had destroyed the living room and attempted to strangle Heather's older brother, who was only nine at the time.

Later in life, Heather was told by her mother that it was the smell of gas that caused the breakdown. I decided to read up on the psychological effects of a gas leak and came across nothing that would invoke a breakdown however, it is known to cause depression and memory loss which are both symptoms related to breakdowns and mania.

Heather said she had to jump out of the window and across to her neighbours. Conveniently, Heathers neighbour was in fact her uncle, so he came around to assist. Heather remembered her father been "knocked out" by him while his wife dialled 999. I asked how her brother was during this and she said that he was "shocked and crying." Her mother was at the shop during the commotion with her older brother and was greeted by one of the officers. Heather's mother had previously worked at the station so knew most of the staff well. She obviously wanted to speak to her husband, but the police refused. He was said to have been sat on the living room floor, crying. Heather described her father in that moment as looking "so small and lost, staring out looking blank."

Heather recalled her father being taken to the local police station first where he gave them his name, rank and number from his time serving in the military. Later that evening, Heather said her father was transferred to High Royds due to a "complete nervous breakdown." This is what Heather was told by the doctor who came to assess her father, as one of the officers on duty that evening had concerns for Ronald. The concerns had come about after her father had only given a few details about himself to the officers. The officers, who had known Ronald, knew he "wasn't dad" according to Heather. That same evening, the doctor had called Heather's mother and informed her what was happening to her husband and that he had been transported to the hospital via patrol car. Heather said that her mother just "sat and cried" when she heard what was happening. At this moment during the interview, she recalled being bullied, alongside her brother, due to her father being in the "nuthouse."

Ronald's first admittance was in 1961, 21 years after his leave from the military. He was given his own room at High Royds when he first arrived and wasn't allowed visitors for the first three weeks according to Heather.

This period of seclusion from family wasn't uncommon in institutions such as this. There's no definitive reason why this was, but most believe that it was done to allow patients to settle and adjust to their medications.

When her mother was eventually allowed to visit, she was told by the staff that Ronald hadn't responded to "usual therapy" so they experimented with ECT. Heather remembers asking her mother what ECT was and she had described it to her as something that "makes his brain jump back to what it should be." Heather wasn't too sure how the staff had explained it to her mother, but she later admitted to Heather that this was the only way she could think to describe it. When I asked what the "usual therapy" was, Heather recalls it being "interaction and talking to a psychiatrist."

Much like other stories which I have come across, the ECT that her father received wasn't consensual, according to her mother, which Heather remembers making her angry.

When Ronald was eventually allowed visitors, he was first seen by only Heather's mother and chaperoned by a ward orderly. The visit was carried out in the doctor's office which Heather described as being at the side of the corridor. Her father was apparently pleading with his wife to let him come home but his cries were cut short when the orderly ordered him to be quiet, saying "she doesn't need to hear things like that." During this meeting, Heather's father was apparently swearing which she described as unusual as her father never swore. The doctor leading the meeting gave a reason for Ronald's breakdown, putting it down to overworking and stress, with the remedy being occupational therapy, ECT and to take each day as it came. Heather's mother had accepted the treatment options as she said, "they knew best."

Through the years, Heather and her mother discussed her father's treatments and time in High Royds, with her mother labelling her husband as being someone who had reformed. "He'd changed and wasn't the man I married" Heather's mother recollected as she thought back to that moment in the doctor's office.

Heather believes that arts and crafts was one of the occupational therapies that the hospital carried out as she remembers her father making "about thirty ashtrays," made from little tiles.

After the first visit, Heather's grandparents came to stay. While Heather and her siblings played outside, the adults sat and spoke in the front room. She is unsure what they were speaking about but could remember her mother crying. "Kids were sort of seen and not heard in those days" Heather told me. She had eventually "snuggled mum," as she described it, but they continued to talk as if she wasn't there.

During many of her mother's visits to see her husband, she noticed a smell around Ronald which they later found out to be Ether.

Ether was an early form of anaesthetic which was used during the mid-19th century. It was a general anaesthetic which means it was more than likely used during ECT treatments. It has been described to be both sweet-smelling and pungent and unpleasant. Ether was inhaled by the patient to render them unconscious however; it was used prior to keep them conscious but pain-free.

During the same conversation, she explained to Heather that her father was "a bit mixed up at the moment."

Visits to High Royds without Heather were common in the beginning, with the relations happening in the doctor's office. I'm unsure if this was common practice to hold visitation outside of the communal areas or it was done given Ronald's current condition. Heather did say that the same office and orderly was used during each visit and this was done so the staff could keep a close eye on him. He was also described as always wearing his night-clothes and unshaven. The persistent smell of Ether was always mentioned by her mother also. I asked Heather is she was given an update after each visit and her mother would give her the same three words, "he's doing okay."

It was Heather's eighth birthday when she was eventually allowed to visit her father in Menston, which was also around four months after his admittance. Her mother had described the hospital as a big palace when speaking about High Royds and "not to be scared." I can only assume an establishment such as High Royds being harrowing for a child, especially the clock tower which elevated above the treeline. Heather's mother had also referred to the hospital as being the "mansion." I asked Heather the reasons behind referring to High Royds as this and she believed it was done as her mother was ashamed that her husband was sent there.

Heather had also asked her mother the same question as a few of the other children at her school had referred to it as the "nuthouse." One of her teachers at school had described the asylum as "a hospital, not for broken bones but for broken minds."

The bottom of the drive was guarded by an officer who had asked her mother who they were intending on visiting. I asked if she remembers seeing any iron gates, but Heather doesn't, however she knew that they were there. Heather started up the main drive and immediately remembered seeing a woman holding a doll, explaining to them that they must stay quite in order not to wake it. She described the drive as being "very long for little legs" but the lawns were "so green" with plenty of flower beds and patients crouched over them. She recalled seeing patients in pyjamas and staff standing alongside them. Some were also seen to be pushing others in wheelchairs. As she approached the administration building, I asked her what she was thinking at that moment and she simply answered with "I'm going to see my daddy."

As they entered the building, they had to empty their pockets while her mother's bag was checked. Shortly after, they were taken to the common room until visitation began. Heather described the room as something you see on TV prison dramas. The room was described as a little café, tea urn on the table with biscuits and tables and chairs also. When visitation began, Heather remembers seeing her father and another six patients file their way through before taking their seats in front of their guests. Heather had not been able to identify her father immediately as she described him as looking like someone from Bergen-Belsen (the concentration camp), with his oversized clothes, sunken eyes and greasy hair. He had begun to speak but only to his wife rather than Heather and her brother. Heather had also brought along a piece of her birthday cake to give to her father but doesn't remember giving him it. She believes she may have sat on it as it was held in her hands. Her mother had told her father that it was Heather's birthday today but it seemed as though it didn't register with him which then resulted with both him and her mother in tears. The only time she remembers her father speaking to her was when he said goodbye. I asked Heather is she tried to speak to her father but she was told by her mother not to speak to him "just in case they upset him."

They had visited Ronald every week after that so they could "get used to him again" as her mother had put it, which prompted her brother to ask "where his real daddy was." Her mother replied, "Daddy is inside that man trying to get out." It wasn't just Heather's brother who was asking that question as Heather told me she was thinking the same thing as they walked back down the drive.

The following week, Heather said she was unable to visit her father as he had been "naughty" according to her mother. He had apparently stood upon his bed and urinated over two orderlies as they attempted to "drag" him off for ECT. During this moment, Ronald's mood seemed relaxed until more orderlies cornered him. This seemingly caused Ronald to become abrupt. "Anything that wasn't nailed down was thrown at them" Heather commented. She stated that during this moment of anger, her father knew exactly what was going to happen to him. When asked how he knew this, Heather said the orderlies liked to tell Ronald he was going for ECT. As a punishment, Heather said her father was confined within a padded cell and made to wear a straitjacket for two days. During his time in the cell, he had told Heather, later down the line, that he had sang to himself, singing every song he knew and repeating the alphabet. He had apparently also attempted to dance but eventually gave up which is understandable since a straitjacket restricts the movements in your upper-body.

As the next week came by, Heather was able to visit it her father again, along with her brothers and mother. This time he had spoken to all of them and admitted he was making sweets for them during his occupational therapy sessions. He had replaced ashtrays with homemade coconut ice, a solid, soft candy coloured pink and white. He was more talkative that week and had reassured Heather that he would be home soon. Ronald still looked unkempt despite his wife taking an electric razor for him to use. It was later revealed that the shaver was taken by another patient. She had offered to help Ronald with a shave and a freshen up, but Heather said the nursing staff had refused this. The fresh clothes that her mother brought in each week had also vanished. Along with Ronald's unkempt look, he also wore nothing on his feet. At this point, Heather mentioned that she smelt first-hand the strong smell of the Ether that was surrounding her father.

A few weeks later, Ronald could visit home for the weekend. A meeting had taken place where Ronald was described as well behaved and labelled as a role model. One of the reasons he was improving in the eyes of the staff, was because he had started taking his medication however, Heather believes her father lied about this. When he arrived home, much like other patients, Ronald brought home his oral medications for the weekend with one of them being a small, red circular one which he dubbed "strawberry fields."

I initially assumed that strawberry fields may have been a sweet that resembled the tablets that Ronald was prescribed however, I only came across a flavouring of Tic-tac's named strawberry fields. I can't say whether these are the confectionary that Ronald was referring to or he just called his pills this to make them seem less frightening to his children.

The tablets that Heather's father took were given to help him sleep. I believe that Ronald was taking Amitriptyline Hydrochloride which presents its self as a small red tablet. This type of medication is an antidepressant; however, amitriptyline (branded as Elavil) can be prescribed in low doses to treat sleeping problems due to it doubling as a mild sedative.

Heather explained to me in more detail what happened the day she found out her father was able to come home for the weekend. It was a Wednesday and her mother was called into High Royds to speak with the doctor overlooking her husband's care. He explained that Ronald had shown vast improvements and would be trialled with home visits. Heather and her brothers were told the news when they returned from school with Heather asking, "is he better now?" Heather's mother had simply replied, "nearly."

The following Friday, Ronald was allowed home and Heather knew the day exactly due to them having fish and chips every Friday for supper. Heather recalled her mother being taken to High Royds by a friend as she didn't have access to a car at that time. They had to wait outside of the administration building until Ronald was brought out by a member of staff.

Heather, along with her brothers, arrived home thirty minutes after her father and was met at the garden gate by their mother who had instructed them to be quite and not disturb their father. Heather said she entered the house and said hello to him in which he responded back. Heather remembered it being "really strange" as "Daddy was home, but he wasn't. Where he was full of life, it was like it had drained away. He was there in body but that's all."

The first evening Ronald was back at the family home, he killed the family cat. The cat had come into the living room from outside, approached Ronald, hissed and arched its back. Ronald had gone to pick the feline up and it, according to Heather, "scratched the hell out of him." In that moment, Ronald had thrown the cat against the wall which caused the rest of the family to begin screaming. The screams were heard by Heather's uncle next door and he immediately came around and grabbed Ronald. He began to cry, apologising to them all for what he had just done. As Heather mourned the cat, her mother quickly tended to his cuts from the cat's claws. Her uncle's wife had followed in moments later and had attempted to calm everyone down but Heather said it didn't work, describing her as a "flapper." After the earlier events had seized, Heather had gone to bed while her parents stayed awake to talk. She remembers her father saying he didn't want to return to Menston.

The following morning, Heather awoke to hear her father tell her he wouldn't be returning to High Royds. He had then taken himself into the back garden wearing just his night-clothes. Heather's mother had followed him out moments later with a mug of tea but he was nowhere to be seen. Her mother had made her way next door to Heather's uncles, but her father wasn't there either. From that moment, Heather doesn't remember what happened, only that the police had arrived at the house later that morning.

Later that same day, her father was arrested and taken back to High Royds. Heather recalled what lead to her father's arrest as her mother had explained the whole scenario that evening.

Her father had apparently walked up New Side Road in Horsforth, making his way towards the Grandways supermarket.

While outside the store, Ronald had thrown a brick through the window and sat until he was arrested. Heather noted that her father had told his wife, during one of his nightly ramblings as Heather described it, that "prison was a better place."

When the police van arrived, Ronald had apparently gone calmly, with no fight, as he thought he was been taken to the station rather than the hospital. It is unsure how Ronald acted while in the back of the van, but based on the fact that he thought he was been taken to the local station, I can only assume that he sat quiet, maybe even feeling happy based on the assumption he wasn't returning to Menston.

Due to the reasons surrounding Ronald's admittance back to High Royds, his wife wasn't allowed to visit him for a long time.

During the time where Heather's mother couldn't visit, she made regular phone calls to High Royds for an update on her husband's care and condition. The only update she was given was that Ronald was having ECT and sleeping a lot. At the beginning of this admission, Heather said no one saw her father for a month.

With the four weeks up, the whole family visited High Royds to see Ronald however; her mother had to see her husband on her own for the first thirty minutes. Heather didn't have the chance to see her father that day as her mother had come out weeping and said they were going home immediately. At the time, Heather wasn't told why they couldn't visit her father, nor why her mother had exited the room crying. It was only years later that her mother had admitted that Ronald was wearing leg irons, commonly known as shackles. These were worn by patients who were at risk of absconding during transportation between locations. I initially assumed that Ronald had attempted to break away from the asylum and this was confirmed by Heather when she informed me that he had tried to abscond from the gardens of the hospital. Heather said that these shackles were used for his own safety. Much like others who were confined to High Royds, Ronald had admitted to Heather that "they were out to get him" but with no one to question the type of care he was receiving, the staff had told his family that he had been diagnosed as a paranoid schizophrenic.

During Ronald's time in hospital, he was denied his War Pension. This led him to the Court of Human Rights where he learnt about his time in the war, a moment he had forgotten.

During his time stationed in Normandy, Ronald and his unit were caught in a crossfire which eventually lead to Ronald being hit. Presumed dead, his Commanding Officer had removed his dog tags and pulled his unit away. The same CO went on record and explained that Ronald was killed in action as he had witnessed it first-hand. Ronald was later found on the field and taken to a local medical area. An envelope was found in his pocket with the word "Leeds" written across the front. As this was the only information they had about Ronald, they transferred him back to the barracks in Leeds. At this point, Ronald had lost his entire memory and was unaware of who he was. During one of the following days, he had made his way into the city centre where he was recognised by a former work colleague who began to shout Ronald's name from amongst the crowd. With Ronald not knowing this was his name, he continued to walk without taking notice before being approached. The gentleman had explained to Ronald of how he knew him and that they had been led to believe he was killed during battle. He was taken back to the barracks where he clarified that he knew Ronald. When he was brought back home, he was given support and guidance which ultimately allowed Ronald to remember life prior to the war and most importantly, his family.

Heather explained this was the reason why he would attempt to escape during his stays in High Royds. Ronald had thoughts that he was back in the war and detained within a prison camp.

Ronald received a pay-out; an apology and his Commanding Officer was later court marshalled. The truth had come out where Ronald had, in fact, taken a bullet to both his back and right leg which caused him to fall and collide with a nearby wall, rendering him unconscious.

After the court hearing, Ronald was required to return to High Royds as Heather's mother had explained that her father was still a danger to himself, others and that he had regressed. Her mother had attempted to seek a second opinion but Heather explained it was difficult in those days. Her mother finally got in contact with the military who stepped in to help Ronald. An army psychiatrist had explained to Heather's mother that the reason for Ronald's regression was due to the ECT treatment he was receiving. He explained that if Ronald was given the correct medication then he wouldn't have needed a lengthy stay in the asylum.

Because of the second opinion and the assistance from the armed forces, Ronald was transferred to the Leeds General Infirmary within four weeks and began to slowly increase his weight. Heather also noted that during his stay in Leeds, he was better kept. Ronald had begun to return to his former self, his mood improved dramatically and he had asked to see Heather and her brothers.

I asked Heather. "How did he seem to you compared to his stay in High Royds" and she merely replied, "oh Ross, I had my Dad back."

Six months later, Ronald had returned to his family home. Heather explained that all he required was the correct medications and reassurance, not straitjackets and ECT. She said that it took him time to readjust to his surroundings and daily routine.

Heather's father passed away peacefully in his sleep four years ago.

***

CLYDE MALLON

1970

Marjorie's account of her husband's stay in High Royds is a mixture of how drugs were used to put a chemical restraint on individuals and how most patients found themselves being admitted and discharged on numerous occasions due to the lack of treatment.

It was the early 1970s and Marjorie's husband, Clyde, had begun to hear voices. Marjorie couldn't tell me what these voices had said to her husband as Clyde never spoke about them, just the fact that they were telling him to do things. Clyde had struggled to deal with the voices, not being able to distinguish if they were real or how others would refer to it as "in his head". Following the voices, Clyde would start "seeing things," referring to cats that he could see roaming around him.

Concerned for her husband's health, Marjorie took Clyde to his GP. The doctor explained to both Marjorie and especially to Clyde, that he would be referring him to High Royds Hospital. Clyde wasn't objecting to this as he apparently knew he wasn't well. Until the admittance, and to reduce Clyde's symptoms, he was prescribed an anti-depressant.

A couple of days after the visit to the GP, an ambulance pulled up outside the house and took Clyde to High Royds. Marjorie noted that during the days following the appointment, Clyde had "really gone downhill and became unwell, to the point where he was unaware of what was happening around him."

Clyde found home in Denton, the ward Marjorie said was for acute admissions and she was instructed not to visit her husband for the first few days as he wouldn't know who she was. She explained to me that this was due to him being "drugged up" and confused.

She brought up two different medications that Clyde was given during his time at High Royds, one was Largactil and the other she referred to as the Modecate Injection.

Largactil was an antipsychotic drug, primarily used in the treatment of schizophrenia. Common side effects were drowsiness, tiredness and blurred vision.

The Modecate Injection was given to individuals who were unreliable at taking their oral medication and would be administered every two to five weeks to maintain symptom control of schizophrenia.

When she was eventually allowed to visit, Marjorie attended each day, sitting beside him in the dayroom.

With Clyde's condition improving, he was able to use the ward's phone to call her his wife. With his health continuing to improve he was then allowed to make calls to Marjorie using the payphone.

During many of her visits to see Clyde, she noted that the doors to the administration building were always opened however; the entrances to the wards were locked and required a buzzer to be allowed in.

During some visits, Marjorie would find herself staying through the patients evening meals. She described the food as "hospital food like today, nothing spectacular but edible." The meals consisted of a three-course meal with the addition of seconds and thirds if available. The staff were quick to offer her a plate for herself and if not, the other patients were quick to offer their deserts they had saved. "Keep them in the fridge until later" Marjorie would answer.

As patients began to show signs of improvement, they were allowed day release from the hospital. Clyde was next to join the list of those showing improvement. He could leave the institution for the day and return in the evening.

With his health showing a continued development, Clyde was allowed home for weekend visits. This would consist of leaving High Royds on Friday evening and returning Monday morning. Marjorie noted that Clyde would bring home his oral medications to take during his stay.

Finally, after spending two months as an inpatient, Clyde was discharged from the care of High Royds and allowed to return back to his family home under the surveillance of his GP and social worker. The discharge came about due to Clyde's improvement after starting the Modecate Injection and the fact that he carried out weekend leave without any issues.

Once back home, Clyde's GP would carry out regular home visits to check his progress. On other occasions, Clyde would attend the GP so he could be given his Modecate Injection and be issued his regular oral medicines.

However, during each discharge, Clyde would relapse. When asked how she knew, Marjorie she said that he would carry out irregular behaviour and become violent. If the manic episode began at home, the GP would be called and would organise another admittance to High Royds or if Clyde was out, the police would be phoned. Marjorie noted that you had to be referred to High Royds; you couldn't just show up on the door. This meant that during some outings, Clyde would be taken to the Accident and Emergency department, with Marjorie ordering the staff to transfer Clyde to High Royds, standing firm and refusing to leave until her wishes were fulfilled. She did recall that during some occasions, the A&E staff weren't interested in helping.

In the lead up to Clyde's second admission, his symptoms returned and he began to hear voices, see the cats and carry out violent behaviour once again. This time, Clyde told his wife that the voices were talking to him, telling him to pick up the kitchen knife. During every relapse, Clyde would take note of Marjorie's face. He insisted that she didn't look like herself, she looked different. The hallucinations that are present with schizophrenia caused Marjorie's face to warp into somebody or something else. Eventually, the GP paid a visit and decided to refer Clyde back to the care of High Royds but this time under sectioning.

Admittance through sectioning was different to voluntary admittance. To be sectioned meant you were at risk of harming yourself and those around you. While under section you can be kept in hospital, stopped from leaving the ward and given treatment without your consent. It also involves a team of professionals assessing you. In this case, Marjorie states that two psychiatrists had to sign the paperwork off.

Moving on nearly ten years after Clyde's first admission and six months after his second discharge from High Royds, he found himself on the edge of his third admittance. He had taken a trip to Leeds City Centre and ambled into one of the many shoe shops the town had to offer. He must have taken interest in a pair of shoes as he attempted to take them without handing over any money. A confrontation must have broken out as Clyde produced a toy gun from his jacket. Because of this, the police were called to the scene. It's unsure whether the police were called because of the attempted theft, the fact that Clyde had pulled out a "fire arm" or the staff recognised his behaviour and feared for his own safety. Either way, he was escorted to Menston and placed back in the care of High Royds.

During Clyde's previous admittances, he was only given treatment using medicines. Marjorie mentioned that during this admittance, Clyde was offered the ECT. There were undoubtedly a lot of reasons why she refused this type of treatment, but she revealed that the firm reason for refusal was due to Clyde having half of his lung removed at Wharfedale Hospital around 1974. "They used to trick you into signing it by sliding another piece of paper alongside it" Marjorie claimed.

After one of Clyde's numerous discharges, he found himself admitted to the Leeds General Infirmary (LGI) after his motorbike collided with an oncoming car. He was diagnosed with "slight brain damage" and also multiple broken bones which removed his ability to walk or talk for a short period of time. He remained in the LGI for a few weeks while they treated his injuries before Clyde suffered another manic episode. The staff had then transferred him over to High Royds to continue his rehabilitation under their care.

As the century began to end, Clyde's admissions continued throughout the 1990s. During the lead up to one of his final admissions, Clyde attempted to strangle Marjorie. This time, Clyde was tried for attempted murder but was found not to be "sound of mind" thus, escorted to High Royds via the police.

This is where Marjorie voiced her concerns for the ward that her husband was admitted to. During the 1990s, roughly thirteen years before the closure of the hospital, the wards began to close with services moving off site. This was evident in the ward where Clyde remained as Marjorie describes the walls as dirty and generally unkempt. It wasn't just the décor that was left to fade, she cited that Clyde was often left unwashed and unshaven however, she never proceeded to raise her concerns. She did, nevertheless, proceed to voice them to a nurse whose response could only be described as "snotty" according to Marjorie. With her concerns still fresh, she decided to call her GP who attended the ward, which is uncommon of a GP, especially when their patient is in the care of another service. The nurse from earlier had been very polite towards the GP which was no surprise to Marjorie.

Roughly twenty years after Clyde's first admission, he was released from High Royds for the final time. He returned to his family home with his wife and his hallucinations would gradually disappear. His occasional outbursts were still present but nothing that warranted another stay in the hospital.

I asked Marjorie if she had anything else to say about the institution, any final few comments in which she goes into below.

Marjorie described the atmosphere on the wards as jolly, staff hastening around without uniforms and poorly patients wandering, dressed in night-clothes amongst the gardens and small shops throughout the self-contained village. She reminisced the Friday night dances in the ballroom and seeing patients walking up to Harry Ramsden's Fish and Chips shop further up Bradford Road. She recalls the restaurant having to remove the vinegar bottles from the outside seating area as the patients would drink them.

When asked about her thoughts on the institution as a whole she referred to it as "the best place to be when you were mentally ill" and that she didn't see any of the bad stigma that was attached to institutions such as High Royds.

There are possibly several reasons for Clyde's recurrent admissions to High Royds. One will have been the use of ineffective treatments of his condition. A relapse on his current medication should have been a sign that things needed to be reviewed rather than repeated. But his pattern of improved behaviour while in High Royds also showed that he may have become institutionalised. You may think that you must be a long-stay patient in order to become labelled as this, but everyone reacts differently. The use of strict routines may have been something that Clyde used to aid his recovery and when being released back into the community the routine disappeared thus, allowing himself to relapse.

***

CLINTON LAM

1970

Elsie's unique story about her brother Clinton is harrowing. The police corruption, the abuse and the affect it had on all of those that were connected to Clinton are everlasting and it goes to show, hidden behind the rules, regulations and the so called 'patient centred care' is the suffering, the torture and the abuse by the staff of High Royds Hospital during a time where the care and vision of the mentally ill had allegedly reformed.

Elsie began her story by telling me how proud she was of her brother. How he himself was a proud and well-respected individual. He was a loving brother and son to his family and that's something that Elsie will never let go of.

It was the mid-1960s and Clinton had just landed his dream job working within the Leeds City Police as a Constable. Further into his career, Clinton was told of an individual who, although known to be a serial criminal, had never been convicted of any law-breaking. He took it upon himself to put this individual behind bars and Elsie knew that her brother would have no problem in achieving this. When Clinton had assembled enough evidence to convict this criminal, he presented his findings to his Senior Officer. To Clinton's surprise, his superior forewarned him that if he continued to involve himself in this case then he could find himself disciplined accordingly. It wasn't just the refusal of the evidence that distressed Clinton, it was the fact that it came from an individual who he admired with great respect. Elsie noted that it wasn't until the late-1960s that the many years of corruption in the Leeds City Police were exposed, attracting the attention of media, not only in the United Kingdom but across the globe.

This was the first time I had come across this corruption which prompted me into research. I came across a post by Neil Wilby, where he writes in great detail about one particular case of police corruption. This is one small extraction from the post,

"Oluwale's death in 1969 was the first known incident of racist policing leading to the death of a black person. It is also the only time in contemporary British history that police officers involved in brutality that directly, or indirectly, led to the death of a suspect have received criminal sentences."

The gentlemen in question, known locally in Leeds City Centre as "Uggy," had also spent time in High Royds Hospital.

I have, alongside other sources of information used, linked this article in the rear of this book.

Due to the dismissal of the evidence, Clinton fled down to London with the intentions of handing over his notes to Scotland Yard, the headquarters of the Metropolitan Police Service. However, Clinton's efforts fell through as he was made aware by a friend that the police were on their way with the aim to detain him on the ground of theft. To this day, the files that Clinton seized have never been found.

When Clinton returned to Leeds, his mental state had deteriorated to a degree where a GP appointment was organised. The outcome of this appointment lead to Clinton being admitted to High Royds Hospital under sectioning.

"My parents were present when my brother was taken away from his home in public view in a straitjacket; my mother in particular was deeply affected by this cruel display of power by the health authority."

This would be the first of several inpatient admissions.

After a brief stay, Clinton was discharged into the care of the psychiatric unit at St. James Hospital. It was here that Clinton befriended a local gentleman named Ronnie. During one of Clinton's outpatient appointments, he and Elsie came into contact with Ronnie's mother who informed them that her son had been admitted to Menston. Troubled by this news, Clinton asked Elsie if she could take him to the asylum to visit him.

Elsie recalled that the visitation between themselves and Ronnie was only allowed in the locked corridor outside of Ronnie's ward and not by his bedside, the dining room or any other room for that matter. Seating in the corridor was non-existent so all three of them had to stand. Ronnie had explained that visitors were never permitted to enter the wards due to the appalling conditions.

I had asked Elsie to describe Ronnie in her own words which she replied with, "he was in there because he was extremely violent, but to me and my brother he was a perfect gentleman."

This quotation sums up just what these individuals were like. Strip away the label of "mental" and you have a decent, ordinary human being who was just like you and I.

Moving back onto the conditions, I also asked if she could describe the setting of High Royds in which she described the corridors as being "frightening, like the pictures you see of the inside of a Victorian madhouse" and that the stench was horrendous. Patients were seen to be roaming the corridor in soiled night-clothes, faeces smeared across the floors and walls like they were mimicking art, walls shedding themselves of its paint, blanketing the scenes of dread below it.

There was one precise dreadful moment that had stuck with Elsie from that same visit to see Ronnie and that memory was of a young gentleman promenading around the halls dribbling repetitively and wearing unbelievably soiled pyjamas. Ronnie had pointed out that this man stood before them was previously an RAF engineer and worked on the grounded planes. One day, a large piece of machinery fell on his head and since then, due to the severe physical trauma, his memory has been wiped and he didn't recognise names, faces and any of his visiting family members, in particular his mother, who Elsie said came each day, travelling from East Yorkshire.

Elsie, in her distressed state, pointed out this gentleman to a passing male nurse and asked if he could assist in getting him washed and changed into clean clothing. The nurse answered with "are you family?" "No" Elsie responded, "then mind your own f**ing business." In response to that, Elsie protested that he deserved more respect however; it seems to have fallen on deaf ears as the nurse walked on. Ronnie had then stepped in and told Elsie to leave it and not to cause a problem. Ronnie went on to explain to Clinton and Elsie the reasons behind the refusal onto the ward. He said the conditions were much worse behind those doors than that of this corridor. Elsie noted that her brother was never placed on the same ward as Ronnie.

Following the abrupt confrontation with the staff nurse, Elsie then proceeded to take a self-guided tour of the grounds with her brother. She remembers seeing some gentlemen, all perched upon deckchairs and all wearing identical straw hats. She gave them a friendly hello; she may have felt like she had to say something if she had caught herself staring at their matching hats. To her surprise, the gentlemen made no attempt to return the greeting, they just sat. They didn't blink, they just stared. Elsie was quick to turn and ask Clinton what was happening and he explained that the gentlemen's blank stares were caused by the tranquilizing effects from their medications and allowed them to remain calm.

During Ronnie's time in the asylum, especially around the late-sixties/early-seventies, the use of chemical restraints had subsided enormously so the effects that these individuals were experiencing may have been one of the many common side effects associated with antipsychotic drugs.

Ronnie later passed away, taking his own life.

During the run up to Clinton's final admission to Menston, he was living in the company of his father near St. James Hospital. Elsie had noticed Clinton becoming more effortlessly agitated over the smallest of things and this would become the first link in a chain of events that had tragic consequences.

It had all begun on a Saturday evening; Elsie remembered receiving a phone call from her brother. His agitation showed on the phone as he asked Elsie to make her way over to his home immediately with some money so he could pay his gas bill. Elsie lived many miles away from her brother and informed him that he would have to wait until Monday to pay his bill but she would call down in the morning to see him. His agitation continued, demanding that he receives the money that evening. She refused to travel on her own in the dark, especially through a neighbourhood that was known to have drug issues. Eventually, Clinton agreed to see Elsie the following morning.

Sunday morning arrived and she made her way over to her father's in hope to find Clinton. As she made her way into the property, there was no sign of her brother, only her father, who appeared to be distressed. Her father had mentioned that two of their relatives had paid a visit and escorted Clinton to the Psychiatric Unit at St. James Hospital. Her father had explained to the relatives that Elsie would be arriving within the next half-an-hour and to leave the decision to her in regards to her brother's state which had arisen from his inability to pay the gas bill.

Nevertheless, despite her father's best efforts, they took Clinton to the hospital and then made their departure, leaving him on his own.

Elsie immediately travelled over to St. James Hospital to be greeted by Clinton sitting on an outside bench enjoying the sun. I can only imagine the huge sigh of relief she gave when seeing him. He appeared much calmer at this moment, just upset that this whole episode resulted in him being at the hospital. After Elsie explained that she had the money for the gas bill, Clinton agreed to go home. This shouldn't have been an issue since his admission to the unit was voluntary. They both proceeded to inform the nurse who was looking after him but to their surprise, the nurse refused Clinton's request to leave as she said they wanted to keep him in for an extra couple of days until he had calmed down. Clinton, of course, disagreed immediately to the nurses remark however, she finally persuaded him to stay.

The following day, Monday, Clinton's father paid him a visit at the hospital. Clinton kindly asked permission to take his father to the canteen for a chat and a cup of tea. Clinton's request was refused however; Elsie mentioned that they had managed to sneak off while the staff were distracted. The next paragraph, in Elsie's words, is claimed to be an eye witness account from the women working in the cafeteria who had gotten to know Clinton over the years of his visits to the psychiatric unit:

Clinton and his father were quietly sitting on their own chatting when two large orderlies (male staff from the unit) came running down to the canteen, shouting and grabbing Clinton before wrestling him to the floor. His father began to protest the violence and the canteen staff noted that the orderlies were being "over the top" with their actions. Knowing his father was witnessing this and would be upset, Clinton tried to halt the violence by struggling to his feet.

It is hard to fathom what was going through Clinton's head while all of this was taking place. The last thing I feel he would have wanted to do while his much-loved father, his role model, watched on, was to give up.

Elsie confirmed that Clinton was transferred over to High Royds the same day.

Later into the day after Clinton's admission to High Royds, Elsie and her father both arrived on site. Clinton was said to be very upset at being back in the asylum after so many years and notified them both that he would be keeping his head down so he could be discharged as soon as possible.

During this conversation, Elsie noticed that her father was staring along the ward and appeared to be fixated on a particular patient. Eventually, he turned to Elsie and explained that he recognised the patient from a previous visit to see Clinton many years prior. Elsie explained that the patient had attacked her father by sneaking up behind him while he was seated and tried to strangle him with a tea towel. Due to this sighting, her father insisted that they reposition their chairs against the walls and proceeded to warn his son to be incredibly watchful when that patient was around. The meeting finally ended with Clinton asking Elsie to bring him some cigarettes during her visit the following day.

What Elsie and her father witnessed the following day is something that no family member should have to see.

They arrived at High Royds and made their way towards Clinton's ward. When she approached Clinton, she saw immediately that he was gravely ill and suspected that he had suffered a heart attack. Clinton had a history of heart complications and had encountered previous heart attacks which allowed Elsie to recognise the signs. Clinton's lips appeared blue, his fingers were unable to bend, his hands had become swollen and they were held stationary in front of his face. Elsie was quick to point out that Clinton had become catatonic and this was evidential as when she proceeded to pass her hands in front of his face, he didn't react. He kept his gaze on the window in front of him. She attempted to give him the cigarettes that he kindly asked for the previous day but he couldn't even form any kind of grip around the packet. Elsie immediately approached the nurse's station and informed him that she believed Clinton was suffering from a heart attack. She was shot down immediately, belittled to say the least. "He is not" the nurse replied, "he had a bit of excitement this morning and fell over on the carpet, that's why his hands are also swollen." This is the reply that Elsie recalled the nurse making. Elise explained how the staff wouldn't accept the diagnosis that she was giving them. She demanded a doctor to come and tend to Clinton and she refused to leave his side until one did. Eventually, with no doctor in sight she, along with her father, were made to leave, two hours after first notifying a nurse. She had to leave Clinton in such a condition that she claims was caused by the neglect of the staff. During the entirety of the visit, Clinton had not communicated with either Elsie or her father. On her exit, Elsie had glanced back to see her brother sat in the front of the window, with his hands held in front of his face, emotionless and fixated on the glass in front of him. Elsie kept echoing the fact that she couldn't do anything to make the staff retrieve a doctor, they just refused and she doubts that a doctor was even contacted that day. She also explained that her father was in a very distressed state, begging his daughter to do something to help her brother, his son.

On the third day of her brother's admittance, I can only envision that Elsie and her father were first through the door when visitation began. Her first sight of her brother showed that his condition had not improved and that encouraged her to make her way over to the nurse's station and confront the staff. She asked what the doctor had said about Clinton's condition but she learnt that no one actually came to see her brother. According to Elsie, the staff informed her that the doctor was unable to make it, he was too busy. In a last gasp effort, Elsie made a call to her own GP using the payphone in the main reception and asked for his advice. With Clinton not being in his care, the GP had no power to change the situation.

Once again, Elsie pressed the staff to contact one of the doctors immediately but much like the day before, the staff brushed off the request. Elsie said that at no point did the staff show any concern for her brother's welfare.

In the early hours of the following morning, Elsie received a call from the Intensive Care Unit at Wharfedale Hospital. They informed her that her brother had suffered a severe heart attack and that she must make her way over as quickly as possible as Clinton's condition was touch and go. Elsie first travelled to her father's home and assisted him with dressing due to his shocked state. They had then made their way to Wharfedale. Elsie noted that at no point had she been contacted by High Royds Hospital to say her brother had been transferred in a critical condition.

On Elsie's arrival, she was taken aback when she encountered Clinton unresponsive. Bruises were obvious on both of Clinton's arms, with further extensive bruising on his ribs, back and legs. With Clinton being under the care of the ICU, he was enveloped in numerous monitoring equipment and receiving oxygen support by the way of a face mask. Elsie had immediately requested information from a senior staff nurse about the bruises that her brother was displaying but was told that all enquires must be directed to High Royds as they were the parent hospital. He continued by instructing Elsie to ask the nurse who resided besides Clinton's bed, a nurse that escorted Clinton from the asylum. Sat besides his bed was an orderly named Carl, the same member of staff that said Clinton had fallen on the carpet back at Menston. Carl was an orderly sent to "keep an eye" on Clinton while he was out of High Royds. Elsie was told that there would be an orderly besides her brother 24 hours a day just in case he became violent. Given her brother's current condition, Elsie couldn't understand why this was necessary. Elsie pressed for answers from Carl who eventually told her that "he fell down the stairs." She didn't believe that for an instant, mainly due to the doors on Clinton's ward being locked for security reasons. "How? The doors are always locked" Elsie answered. Carl then became verbally aggressive, accusing her of calling him a liar and refusing to give her a valuable answer.

The staff at Wharfedale accommodated for both Elsie and her father, providing a bed for him in a nearby room, close to his son's unit. Elsie remained by Clinton's bedside for the remainder of the night, with Carl leaving the ward on a regular basis, purchasing beverages for himself. Elsie noted that Carl never spoke to her and any questions she did put forward were ignored.

The following morning, around six, Clinton finally regained consciousness but immediately became hysterical when his confused gaze met Carl. He immediately became inconsolable, frantically pointing at the orderly, screaming "he's the hitman sent to kill me!" It wasn't long until the orderlies had switched places and Clinton would return to his calm state. When Carl later returned, Clinton's behaviour took a sudden turn; he would be pulling at his leads, attempting to leave his bed, shouting the familiar words "don't let him kill me!" Carl, unfazed, was quick to respond with "don't be stupid."

At this point in the interview, Elsie thanked Wharfedale for the care they gave her, especially giving her father a room close to Clinton, so he could stay overnight and not be too close to witness what his son was experiencing.

During one of the usual tea rounds, Clinton was asked if he would like a cup of tea. Carl was quick to refuse on behalf of Clinton. He refused as he believed that Clinton would throw the hot cup of tea towards him, staining his nice clean shirt. During this moment, two friends arrived to see Clinton and one of them remonstrated heatedly with Carl who explained that he was in charge and they should "keep out of it."

Elsie continued to mention her brother's fear of Carl. His nightmare, perhaps a recurrent one that had made its way from the halls of High Royds to Wharfedale Hospital, sat beside his bedside.

After seeing her brother's reaction repeated every time Carl entered the room, she made a request to the Senior Nurse of the ICU that the orderly not be sent to sit beside her brother. However, even though they had witnessed the affect Carl was having on Clinton, they instructed Elsie to send all requests to High Royds. Continuing with his reactions whenever Carl clocked in for his shift, Elsie's family members who visited Clinton regularly at Wharfedale also noticed how hysterical Clinton became when Carl was watching over him.

Eventually, a new orderly, by the name of George, came to sit beside Clinton. There were three regular orderlies that worked on a rota basis but George was a new face to Elsie in which she described him as "very pleasant."

Elsie's frustration regarding Carl continued to boil over for the next few days as she was at war with staff to prevent her brother from returning to High Royds once he was discharged from the care of the ICU. Elsie requested that Clinton be transferred to the Coronary Care Unit (CCU) at St. James Hospital, a more appropriate place for Clinton due to his on-going heart complications. Her frustrations didn't just stop there, she was aching over the fact that no one was admitting that something terrible had happened to Clinton and how he could sit there, dormant, lifeless in front of those windows for three days while he had a heart attack.

She approached George and demanded that he told her everything she needed to hear. George began by clarifying that he had a mortgage and two young children at home to support and by revealing information about Clinton's injuries, he could lose his job. Elsie continued to push for answers, reassuring George that she wouldn't reveal her source of this information. He also made it clear that if this matter was taken to the courts and he was summoned as a witness, then he would deny anything Elsie had claimed he said. He confirmed that the bruises and injuries that Clinton had sustained were caused by Carl. According to George, Clinton had been sitting in this chair at Menston when Carl collided with him, sending him onto the floor. He had then seemingly continued to beat Clinton. George said that Carl had approached Clinton and issued him an order, whether Clinton didn't hear him, or answered with something that Carl didn't appreciate. As this fell on deaf ears, George explained that Carl "went for him." He explained to Elsie that Carl was hoping that Clinton wouldn't pull through, resulting in the abuse being covered up as well as the fact that no medical assistance was given to Clinton when it was clear it was urgently desired. Shortly after, Clinton suffered a serious heart attack and was blue-lighted to Wharfedale Hospital and stationed in the ICU. George finished by explaining that none of the staff on the ward had any knowledge of Clinton's on-going heart issues.

Elsie eagerly awaited Carl to swap with George so she could confront him. Once Carl had taken his seat beside Clinton, Elsie attacked him, repeatedly asking what had happened to her brother and she recalled saying "he looks like he's had a good kicking" and Carl quickly changed his story. Elsie remembered Carl telling her "there was a point where Clinton made an unprovoked attack on me and had to be restrained." The staff claimed at the time that they were not aware that this attack had brought on a second heart attack which later resulted in a third which was much worse. Elsie rubbished this excuse as George was aware of her brother's heart complication so why weren't the others? She continued by saying she felt the ward team were intimidated by Carl, afraid of him almost.

As Clinton's stay in Wharfedale continued, so did his paranoia. His theory of a hitman grew uneasily and every unrecognisable visitor that approached his bedside placed him into a mode of panic. In Elsie's words, he was petrified of them.

Elsie's wishes to move her brother to the care of St. James Hospital was finally approved as the staff on the Intensive Care Unit came to an agreement with one of the consultants at the CCU. The move was given the go-ahead and Clinton was eventually transferred over to the Coronary Care Unit at St. James Hospital.

The nurses in the CCU at St. James Hospital tended to his needs sensitively and had even placed a mattress on the floor of the patients' lounge, next to the nurse's station so he would feel safe and protected throughout the night. However, his mental state continued to worsen as he began to talk about assassination rather than a hitman when family and friends visited.

Elsie explained that even though Clinton's mental state had begun to significantly decrease, the consultant would not be transferring him to the attention of the Psychiatric Unit until he was entirely convinced that the care he received there was severely more adequate than that of the CCU.

Clinton's father, as usual, continued to attend the CCU unit to see his son.

On one such day, Clinton's father and himself had talked besides his bedside until Clinton stood up, telling his father he would be back in a moment. His father's suspicions began to arise when Clinton failed to return from wherever he had ventured to. His father immediately began to search for him and since he was unable to locate him, he informed one of the nurses and they initially concluded that he may have wandered off site and walked home which was very close to the hospital. The staff had then organised a taxi to take Clinton's father home while they informed the hospital's security.

The final part of this story is daunting. It truly shows how a patient with mental illness suffers, and in some, the on-going nightmare in which they live.

Clinton had indeed headed home, back to a place where he thought he would be safe. Unfortunately, he was unable to enter his home as he had no key. His next-door neighbour had spotted him from her window, wearing only his socks and hospital pyjamas. She had quickly invited him in and attempted to warm him up by making a pot of tea. According to his neighbour, it was only a short time after that she heard the sound of a car screaming to a halt at the foot of Clinton's home. His neighbour approached the gentlemen who exited the car and was confirmed to be a plain clothes officer in an unmarked police vehicle. She explained that Clinton was with her inside. At this moment, Clinton had entered into a stage of extreme panic; he headed for the stairs, screaming that the assassin had located him.

His frantic behaviour continued as he began barricading the attic door with furniture. The police officer, who had unnecessarily barged past his neighbour, stood on the reverse of the door, instructing Clinton to come out. His father arrived and made his way towards his son but the police refused to allow him to attempt any communication. Elsie explained that she later found out the reason behind the police's refusal was due to Clinton supposedly threatening to kill his father with a knife. Elsie immediately refuted this as the relationship between father and son was one of mutual love and respect, her brother would never have made such threats.

Clinton continued to scream from behind the attic door, refusing to release himself. Elsie explained that she believed the unmarked police car added to her brother's increasing fears. His inability to recognise it as a police vehicle heightened his uncertainties. He threatened to set the barricade on fire if the "assassin" attempted to get past. The police dismissed his warning, reassuring themselves that it was an empty threat but it wasn't, with no fire brigade or ambulance summoned and Clinton becoming more frightened and isolated, he set the furniture alight, along with many toxic black plastic bin liner bags, using the lighter from his pyjama pocket.

It was only when the smoke began to appear under the door that a call to the fire service was made. On arrival, they called for an ambulance crew to assist.

Clinton was finally retrieved from the fire and blue lighted to A&E. While in transit, Clinton suffered another major heart attack.

That particular day, Elsie had organised to visit Clinton in the afternoon but had been delayed at work. It was only when she went home to retrieve some paperwork that she encountered her answerphone maxed with voice messages. They all gave an identical message, get to the A&E urgently.

By the time Elsie had arrived, Clinton had been transferred to the Intensive Care Unit and fitted with a ventilator. He remained unconscious, with the burns from the blaze displayed clearly. She had made the effort to reach under his blanket in an attempt to hold his hand but the nurse immediately pulled her away. She explained that Clinton's hands had been destroyed in the fire, maybe through an attempt to drown the flames with his hands. Elsie remained by his side, allowing her father a chance to see his son but understandably, he couldn't process what he was seeing. He made the point that he could see Clinton's chest rising and falling which put him under the impression that he was going to recover but unfortunately this was the work of the ventilator.

Clinton later passed away.

Elsie found it difficult to describe Clinton's last moments, but she uttered the words, "he stilled looked handsome to me."

After the passing of his son, Clinton's father resided with Elsie as he couldn't face returning to the home he once shared with his son, nor live next door to the house which was still visibly damaged from the blaze. His struggles with the stares led him to apply to the Housing Association for a new permanent home. He applied for sheltered housing accommodation nearer to his daughter and due to the circumstances surrounding him, the move was authorised swiftly. Elsie said that this was an enormous plus for her as her current occupation took her away from home for numerous days a week so this allowed her worries of her father to subside. She admitted that her father missed Clinton dreadfully, reminiscing memories of him on each of her visits to see him.

Elsie's concerns for Clinton's suffering caused by the staff members of High Royds were still at the forefront of her mind. She wanted answers about the physical abuse he encountered which caused a needless heart attack and later, a more severe one. She took her initial concerns to the head of the mental health unit in Leeds, who advised her that any complaint would not be dealt with for at least two years while investigations were undertaken and stressed the fact that this would cause her and her father a lot of distress.

The head also explained that due to lack of evidence in these cases, this would be a major factor in no action taking place against the accused.

At this point, Elsie reintroduced George into our conversation. She said she never wanted to call on him as a witness, to "drag him into this mess" but if it meant getting justice for her brother, she would seriously consider it. Her father wasn't happy at the idea of submitting a formal complaint against the asylum and she remembered him telling her that "this won't bring Clinton back." However, against his wishes, Elsie wrote a letter of complaint but regrettably, due to the potential stress it would induce on her father, she never posted it. It continues to sit there, holding questions to answers that Elsie and her father, may never get.

"I never really got over the fact that justice wasn't served" Elsie finished.

Her father sadly passed in 1997, still grieving the loss of his son.

I continued to talk to Elsie about High Royds as a whole, speaking about her perception of the place.

I asked her what she thought it was like within those wards, the atmosphere and the treatment of the patients. She recalled a lot of bullying and aggressive behaviour happening on the ward her brother was stationed and felt that if she spoke up about her concerns of Clinton's care too often, then they, (presumably the staff,) would take it out on him and make his stay, on any consequent admittance, worse than the last. "I basically kept my mouth shut to keep him safe" she said.

Clinton was loved by his father, his sister and many others, continuing to be present in the minds of those for the remainder of their lives.

***

HAROLD CHAPMAN

1970

Harold Chapman's admission came after a series of family deaths. Those who carry a lot of grief on their shoulders eventually break, unable to cope with the memories and feelings they have supressed for so many years.

Heather's husband was thirty when his suppressed feelings and emotions got the better of him.

It had all begun after his grandmother passed away which was closely followed by the death of his grandfather and finally his mother, all within the space of two and a half years. It wasn't until eight years after the death of his mother when Harold's emotions got the better of him. Heather described her husband as "very controlling and a very large child." They had eventually split after he "fell apart."

After the split, Heather had returned to her mother's house but it wasn't long after that Harold had turned up at her door step. He arrived in tears but was met by her mother as Heather was at work at the time. For whatever reason, Heather said that her mother had taken Harold to see the GP who, in the end, decided to have him admitted to High Royds that same day. It's not clear the reason for Harold's admission but due to the recent split on top of his family deaths, I can only assume it was due to severe depression.

Heather said that her mother had called her while she was at work to inform her what had happened. According to Heather, when she spoke on the phone to her mother, she had just told her that he was ill and had taken him to the GP. Heather described her mother as old school so she didn't talk much about why he was crying or what had happened. This was a common reaction to mental health during the mid-1900s. Those who were suffering from mental illnesses were often not spoken about. To some, it was an embarrassment to have family members suffering like this. Heather expanded on this by telling me that her mother never elaborated on the use of the word ill because "it was not something she would have talked about because of the stigma of mental illness."

Heather and her father travelled to High Royds with Harold that evening. I asked Heather how Harold seemed to her when she arrived home and she described him as "vacant, he just resigned." Harold's mood continued like this throughout the journey to Menston. At this point during the interview, Heather recalled a moment where they attended the GP. This appointment was attended when Harold was in his early sixties, and the doctor diagnosed him as mildly autistic which would explain his breakdown, not being able to cope with changes (her leaving and the family deaths.)

During the first stage of her husband's admission to High Royds, Heather vaguely remembered him being on a small ward with only four beds but she can't be sure. Harold was shown to his bed while Heather was asked numerous questions about Harold. She described these as awkward since they had separated. An example she used was "Did he have any bruises?" While the questions were being asked, Heather noted that her husband contributed very little. After Harold had settled in, Heather left.

She remembered that the patients were allowed a little money for the phone and that gave Harold the chance to call her. She said that she would receive phone calls every day and found them difficult to handle, mostly because Harold would be crying and pleading to come back home. She put across that it was often difficult to calm him down. He always used to say the phrase "I want to come home" but Heather didn't know what home was, her mother's or their marital home. Harold continued to tell Heather that he didn't like it in High Royds.

However, Heather said that things began to change for the better when he became involved with a group, which Heather described as alcoholics, who could leave the ward and attend the local pub. It's unclear what pub Harold sauntered to as I have no knowledge of the taverns around High Royds during the 1970s. Heather, still to this day, can't understand why patients were allowed to attend the local inns.

From then on, Heather explained that Harold's crying down the phone stopped. He still wanted to come home but wouldn't be as agitated about the fact that he couldn't. She also mentioned that when he became restless, the staff would allow him to play the piano which, according to Heather, calmed him down.

A few weeks after Harold's admittance, he could leave the hospital on a Friday night and stay at Heather's mothers. He would then return Monday morning. During his weekend visits, Heather described him as settled.

Heather told me that she would visit him every weekend, either with her father or brother who would drive her down. During one of the visits, at a point where Harold was allowed off-site, they took a trip over to Harry Ramsden's for lunch. Heather described Harold eating as if he was starving but it later came out that he didn't remember going.

She explained that each visitation was held in the dining room and if he was coming home for the weekend, they would meet him outside of the main entrance. Heather recalled one weekend when she took Harold to Otley for a walk down the river.

Harold was given Electroconvulsive Therapy during his stay in High Royds alongside other oral medications. I asked Heather how her husband seemed after ECT and she described him as "rather zombie like." She said that he could remember things from "way back" but nothing as recent as the week before. Heather doesn't remember giving consent for the procedure so can only assume that Harold gave it. When asked about any physical trauma signs, Heather doesn't recall seeing anything, no scaring or burns. Harold had never explained to Heather how the ECT happened and if it helped him. He was given five or six treatments during his six-week stay but Heather believed that it wasn't effective. She did mention that Harold used his ECT treatment as an excuse whenever he forgot anything.

When the discharge date came, Heather didn't remember how it came about or what it entailed, she only remembered being told that he could go home. I asked if she ever received any discharge advice from the hospital but she doesn't recall receiving any.

During the time Harold was in High Royds, Heather was in the middle of purchasing a new home for herself so when Harold was discharged, he came to live with Heather and they gave their relationship another go. Heather stated that the relationship was awkward when he moved back in, "Harold wanting to dictate" is the way she described it. He had mentioned to her that after only three weeks back home, he didn't enjoy living there so she told him he could move out but that she was staying. "I never wanted to buy another house in my life."

Harold was out of work for a long period after his discharge and couldn't sleep without his sleeping tablets that High Royds prescribed him. She explained that it took a long time to wean him off them, starting by giving him herbal ones then moving onto paracetamol. She still described him as "controlling. His way or the wrong way" and admitted that she had been a "real mouse." She was afraid of him but learnt to stand up for herself. Harold would eventually return to work but had difficulties settling in as every time there was a change it would take him a while to adjust. This may have been down to his mild autism.

Sadly, Harold later passed away in 2018 of heart failure and cancer. 44 years after his discharge from High Royds.

Due to the wide spectrum of mental health disorders, Harold was caught between two diagnoses, autism and depression. The wide variety of mental illnesses means it is sometimes difficult to diagnose someone until other symptoms appear.

***

ED BOLTON

1972

Adele gave me a short account of her father's time in High Royds and how he was trialled with a variety of medications and treatments during his short stay in 1972.

She remembered her father's illness beginning slowly. At the time, her father, Ed Bolton, was employed as an ambulance driver and later became diagnosed with manic depression, or as we know now, bipolar disorder.

The diagnosis came after Adele's mother had taken Ed to the doctors where she explained about her husband's episodes. After the diagnosis, I asked Adele if her father was ever aggressive but she denied he was, only claiming that he wanted lots of noise, or a lot to be happening around him during one of his episodes. She gave examples such as having the TV volume turned up and occasionally playing the violin at the foot of her bed at two in the morning.

She explained how during one of his shifts as an ambulance driver, he and his best friend were called out to a traffic collision where a young boy had been hit by a vehicle. The dispatch team quickly came to realise that the child involved in the accident was actually Ed's colleague's son. At this point, Adele explained that it was too late to call them back to the station.

The accident may have been the first trigger for Ed's mental health decline and the funeral that he attended may have also added to his decay.

Shortly after the funeral, Adele said her father's behaviour at work changed, refusing to attend emergency calls and insisted on remaining at the depot cleaning ambulances. This behaviour is not uncommon, set aside from the fact that Ed had bipolar disorder; he could have been suffering from PTSD.

Ed's admission to High Royds came on Adele's birthday, 6th October 1972. She said that her father was expecting to be admitted as he sat patiently, sporting his hat and coat, presumably in the front lounge of his home. Adele also mentioned that there had been discussions previously, around a couple of years prior, that Ed would voluntary attend High Royds but I can only speculate that nothing came of it. Before her father was escorted out, Adele was sent upstairs and made to remain in her room, only remembering her father stood on the doorstep, alongside her mother who wept. A car had appeared shortly before carrying two doctors.

During his stay, Adele remembered her father being given Lithium.

Adele told me that medication was "hit and miss" in the 1970s.

In the 1960s, bipolar patients weren't given much help as the government refused to acknowledge bipolar disorder as an actual illness.

Ed was also known to have had ECT while at the hospital, which Adele remembered having no affect, regardless of the amount of times he received it. But like most of those who had ECT, Adele noted that her father had become quiet and "slow." She recalled him being a quiet man in general but the new shade of quiet that he had inherited was different. He had become very withdrawn and only acting out or being loud during one of his manic episodes which he continued to have during his inpatient stay. Talking loudly and swearing was Ed's most common behaviours during his episodes according to Adele.

I asked her if she could remember any details of Denton and she explained that they had a day room for visitation or, for those who were unable to, they would have their visits at their bedsides or within a private room. Adele mentioned that some of the visits she attended were carried out by the bed space due to Ed's episodes. If her father was having a bad day, Adele admitted that she wouldn't stay long however, her mother did visit weekly from Armley.

Ed eventually self-discharged during his first admission, which Adele believes was around two years, before returning under section. She didn't mention the reason behind her father's second admittance.

With Ed being diagnosed at a time where medication was slowly being introduced into asylum life, he ultimately found himself confined to the asylum. It's hard to say whether Ed could have avoided a stay in the hospital, even with the introduction of antipsychotics, as High Royds continued to admit patients until around the 1990s, regardless of the advancements in psychiatric care.

***

EMILY SILVA

1979

Beth's mother, Emily Silva, had suffered multiple distressing situations that began early in her childhood. These several occasions may have been a factor in her admittance to High Royds in 1979.

Beth began by explaining that her mother suffered from depression for a number of years prior to her admittance to Menston, being prescribed numerous anti-depressants and sleeping tablets.

Beth's mother and her three sisters had been abused during their childhood by a member of the family which Beth believes happened when her mother was around five years old. Emily's grandmother stepped in and took all three sisters to the doctors to be examined. According to Beth, the doctor had told Emily's grandmother to keep quiet about the abuse in which she refused. She went on to contact the courts to get a restraining order on the accused family member to prevent them from entering the house where the three sisters resided.

In 1969, Emily had unfortunately given birth to stillborn twins with her husband.

It is believed Emily's depression began when her children returned to school following the holidays. Emily had taken to one of the sister's dolls and would take it walking with her during the night, wearing nothing more than her nightwear.

While this was happening, Beth explained that her father was a train driver which meant he would spend long periods of time away from home. She also explained that he had a fear of his wife's mental illness so he would dismiss it.

It is unclear when, but Emily eventually had a breakdown in which Beth believes was caused by herself and her sisters leaving home, all three within a short period of time as they all had become newly married.

A child leaving home is a common trigger for many feelings such as sadness, grief and loneliness. These feelings can leave individuals vulnerable to developing depression. Parents who feel these emotions are dubbed to have Empty Nest Syndrome.

In Emily's case, she may have felt these emotions and if left unresolved, may have developed into depression which triggered her breakdown.

During her mental collapse, Beth explained that a doctor had travelled to see her mother from Scotland for a home visit, alongside her mother's regular GP. She was then led to the car parked outside which was destined for the asylum. Beth explained that this admission was deemed as an involuntary sectioning. It appears as if Emily was sectioned against her wishes due to her mental state.

Beth also noted that her mother had previously suffered from occasional blackouts which she said was later linked to abnormal brainwaves.

Many individuals have an electroencephalogram, or EEG, every year which is a test to see if the brain is functioning correctly. An abnormal EEG outcome can result from a number of causes, including epilepsy and seizures. Blackouts can be caused by epileptic seizures or even psychogenic seizures which is an event that resembles an epileptic seizure, but without the characteristic electrical discharges associated with epilepsy. Unfortunately, I can't confirm if this was the causes for Emily's blackouts.

Emily's admission to High Royds came around 1979, with Emily herself being around 44 years of age.

She didn't comment on what ward her mother was housed on, but based on her short period in the institution and a less severe prognosis, I believe

Emily resided in the admissions block of the hospital. Based on the year she was admitted, I would say she was stationed in the Beamsley Block.

Beth described the conditions of the hospital as "horrible. Doors were kept locked; patients were walking around with that much medication in them they looked like they were sleep walking."

Beth continued to describe the environment, noting that the place was "very noisy" which was caused by the patients' continuous shouting and disruptive behaviour. She also recalled a woman "banging her head against the wall."

She described the staff as being "very dismissive," explaining that it was very difficult to pull any information from them in regards to the treatment her mother was receiving.

During the early days of Emily's stay, Beth explained that "it was scary initially, not knowing what to expect but it became normal after a few visits."

Further into her visits to see her mother, she remembered witnessing her mother tucked beneath a table, clutching a baby doll which she described as being "heart-breaking to see."

During her stay in the establishment, Emily was subject to the controversial ECT treatment which Beth didn't recall having to give consent for. Based on the fact that Emily was sectioned, the therapy could have been given without her consent if the doctors deemed it necessary. Emily did say however, that after the treatment, her mother came across as more improved.

Emily was housed in the asylum for six months before being discharged, returning to her family home with no medications. Her care wasn't halted there as she continued as an outpatient for two years.

After her mother returned home, she explained that she was able to block out any future stress and the only signs of her time in the asylum were the temple scaring that she showcased from her ECT sessions. Emily was able to remember most of her time before her admittance but her short-term memory had become affected after the therapy.

Beth went on to admit that both her, her daughter and niece had all been diagnosed with bipolar which leads her to believe that her mother may have suffered the same illness.

Finally, Beth explained that her childhood was a happy one, with her mother's illness not affecting her or her sisters.

Emily was, according to her daughter, another example of a positive outcome from ECT. To be discharged from the asylum after six months with no remittances shows that to some, ECT was the solution.

***

LINN BAKER

1980

Linn Baker's short account, with the help of her husband, gives details on how postnatal depression was perceived in the 1980s.

Linn's mental health had seemed to decline after she gave birth to baby Daniel. Two weeks later, she was discharged home but had plans to return in four weeks for her postnatal exam.

During postnatal exams, you are commonly asked about how you are feeling as part of a general discussion about your mental health and wellbeing, as well as a general physical check-up.

The postnatal exam was carried out at Hyde Terrace Hospital. I attempted to research the old hospital but found very little information which is surprising. I believe that the hospital stood on the site where The Mount currently resides and was closed down around 1984 when it merged with another maternity ward at the Leeds General Infirmary. This information was the only evidence I could find of Hyde Terrace Maternity Hospital.

At this point during the interview, Linn's husband, Bruce, stepped in as she wasn't able to remember much of her time after Daniel's birth.

I am unsure how soon Linn's mental health deterioration was picked up after the appointment as Bruce remembered her "flipping out" after the exam but didn't give details on how soon after.

He explained that his wife began to act very "irrationally and out of character." He continued by saying that she felt very insecure and lost any sense of reason. Linn had apparently got worse over a three-week period, presumably three weeks after her exam.

A week before Linn's health was at its worse; she had begun to smell things that weren't present.

Her climax came when Bruce left her and Daniel with his parents while he was out playing football one afternoon. Shortly after, he stopped by to check on Linn after his parents raised their concerns to him. He admitted that she "wasn't the woman I knew." I asked Bruce what kind of behaviour she was exhibiting and he explained that she was asking for cigarettes even though she had never smoked. He also went on to explain that Linn had begun showing signs of auditory hallucinations (hearing sounds, but the sounds are not actually there), hearing voices and imagining that she was on TV. He also explained that the voices she was hearing was telling her to "come back to normality." Linn was also known to have seen the ghost of her dead brother. She admitted that the apparition didn't speak to her but came across in a ghostly way, the way they are portrayed on television and in movies.

Linn finally began to settle but remained in a dazed state with Bruce saying she had a "crazy look in here eye." He took her back to their home but come midnight, she presented with her second case of mania, trashing the bedroom and attempting to thrown herself from the second-floor window. Bruce had eventually restrained her before calling the out of hours GP service and locking the windows.

"It was awful seeing my gentle wife turn into a monster."

When the doctor arrived at the house, Linn had acted out and bit him which caused him to refuse to see to her unless she was "pinned down." While she was being restrained, the doctor gave her an injection to render her unconscious, seemingly Benzodiazepines which act as a sedative, and placed her on a stretcher, bound for High Royds.

All of the behaviours that Linn presented can be features of diseases such as Schizophrenia, Bipolar Disorder and other disorders. One rare psychological illness that can present itself after child birth is postpartum psychosis. This mental illness is serious and can affect new mothers. It usually starts within a few days or weeks after giving birth, and can develop suddenly, within just a few hours. I am not suggesting that this is what Linn was suffering from, but these are just a few of the illnesses linked to her behaviours.

Linn didn't remember her admittance to High Royds and she admitted she "totally lost the next four weeks." Her husband was informed not to visit for the first couple of days, much like most families are told, in which he listened.

Bruce was only able to recall the odd memories, the first one being that he had to move into his parents' house so he was able to visit Linn without taking Daniel along and that Linn had asked him to sneak her out of the hospital.

Bruce recalled his wife resembling a zombie during her stay in the institution, "totally off the planet and delusional" is how he described her. He remembers her attempting to escape on multiple occasions and also took it upon herself to steal other patients' slippers and belongings.

At the beginning of her stay, Linn was given medications for around four weeks in which Bruce said she didn't respond to, so they went ahead and gave her multiple sessions of ECT. Bruce admitted that this "brought her back to being the Linn that I knew." This leads me to believe that when he described Linn as being zombie-like, he was referring to the time before her ECT took place.

Linn was given six treatments of the therapy during her short stay, with her husband explaining that each session used 10,000 volts and was given twice a week for three weeks. Bruce's figure of the voltage used is quite incorrect. The voltage of a typical house in the UK is 230 volts so Bruce's figure is enough voltage to power around 43 homes. The actual voltage used in an ECT session could be anywhere between 70 and 450 volts with the bursts of electricity being administered for as little as 0.1 seconds.

Linn was only a short stay patient, and remained as an inpatient for eight weeks. A week after her final session she was allowed to return home. Bruce explained that once Linn had begun receiving the ECT she gradually got better, with promising signs beginning after the first session.

Nothing more was said after that so I presume that after Linn's discharge she resumed her normal life, raising baby Daniel with her husband with little or no concerns regarding her mental health.

Linn suffered her postnatal depression at a time where women were confined to the asylum because of this very diagnosis. Today, Linn's grief may have been treated with counselling rather than an inpatient stay and prescribed an antidepressant.

***

NORMA FRENCH

1980

April's mother, Norma French, is an example of an individual who became institutionalised and also became a failed member of care in the community. Due to her constant battle with depression and suicidal thoughts, Norma encountered several inpatient stays at the asylum.

Norma had married young and seized working to be a stay-at-home house wife as well as a full-time mother. Prior to her marriage, she used her upholstery skills to make dresses which April said she seemed to enjoy. April explained that women were prone to become stay-at-home wives after marriage back then, which I believe would have been around the mid-1950s, early 60s.

April described her mother as a quiet woman and always kept to herself.

Norma's mental health began to decline when April was sixteen and it was during this time when she began self-harming.

Originally, Norma was sent to Scalebor Park, an asylum that resided in Burley in Wharfedale, with her first admittance coming around the 1980s.

Scalebor Park was the first asylum to be built in the West Riding of Yorkshire and opened in 1818. Due to overcrowding issues, it was decided that further asylums would open across the county with Wadsley Park opening in Sheffield in 1862, followed by High Royds in 1888 and finally, the fourth and final asylum at Storthes Hall being planned from the start of the 20th century. Scalebor Park began to downsize towards the end of the 1900s as care in the community was the focus moving forward. Scalebor

Park finally closed in 1995 but a small service, Moor Lane Centre, maintained its respite services until spring 2009.

It was not clear how long Norma was housed in Scalebor Park as April mentioned that her mother had been in and out of inpatient care over a ten-year period.

While Norma resided in Scalebor Park, she was taking a variety of medications. It's hard to say what medication Norma was given in the 80s, but it appears that Chlorpromazine, known more commonly under the brand name Largactil, was the choice of drug during the later 1900s however; I can't say for certain this is what Norma was prescribed.

After she was discharged, Norma would continue on her medications however, according to April, her mother would stop taking them. She mentioned that most individuals suffering from paranoid schizophrenia, such as her mother as I later found out, would eventually stop taking their tablets.

Eventually, Norma was referred to High Royds by her GP. April didn't say the reason behind the admittance, but based on her history of self-harm, I can only assume this was the motive.

April described High Royds as being a "rehab centre" for her mother as she was only placed in their care in order to get her back onto her medications. This may have been the case as she remembers Norma being housed in the Beamsley Block which was the admissions ward and sometimes housed short stay patients. A strict routine of medication times and being given the tablets in a controlled setting meant Norma had no other option but to begin her medicines again.

I asked April how long her mother was kept in High Royds during each admittance and she believes it was only a few weeks at a time, with the longest inpatient stay being six weeks.

After Norma was back on her medications, she was allowed to be discharged and sent back to her place of stay. April mentioned that during her mother's time, there was no care in the community so patients were left to care for themselves unless they had family members on hand.

April explained that each admission and discharge was the same for Norma, returning home, taking her medication that High Royds placed her on before stopping and being re-admitted into their care.

I asked April how her mother was re-admitted each time and the reasons behind the repeated stays. She explained that each admission was most commonly from the local A&E as Norma had repeatedly attempted suicide but thankfully, for April, failed.

After each discharge, April remembered not seeing any significant improvement in regards to her mother's condition, but then again, High Royds merely played the role of a mother, making sure their child, Norma in this case, took her tablets and did as she was told. April also noted that each admission that her mother encountered was voluntary, that is until her final stay where the GP threatened to section Norma unless she went on her own accord. April confirmed that she did.

Due to each admission being linked to self-harming, I asked April why she believed her mother continued to inflict injuries upon herself and she confirmed that she believed it was a cry for help.

During her stays, Norma enjoyed the company that she encountered in her dormitory; this was because on the outside, she didn't have any companions. April said her condition, her illness, stopped her from interacting with people. In High Royds, most patients share the same illness so this allowed Norma to freely connect with others without the fear of being judged.

When it came to visitation, April would visit twice a week from her home which was a 22-mile round trip by car. She recalled being allowed to visit her mother's bedside but she opted to take her for a walk around the grounds instead. If the weather was bad, or if they preferred to stay indoors, April would take her mother to the ballroom which she described as being thick with smoke from the patients smoking, to the point where you couldn't see through.

April herself, remembered a few distinct characters during her visits to High Royds, with one being an elderly gentleman who had resided there since the war in the 1940s, that war being World War II. The gentlemen in question had suffered shell shock.

Many believe that shell shock is caused by an exposure to shell bursts however; it was proven that soldiers who weren't on the front line also suffered similar symptoms, these being anxiety, nightmares, heart palpitations, depression and many others. Doctors came to the conclusion that it was caused by exposure to stressful situations.

The gentlemen would be seen picking up tab ends from the ground and placing them in his pockets which would cause his trousers to become alight. According to April, the gentleman hadn't spoken since he suffered the shell shock.

Another memory that April conjured up was in regards to the severity of the patient's conditions. She said that the more ill the patients were, the further they were placed up the corridors. In a way, April was correct in saying this as the patients who had a poor prognosis were confined to the chronic blocks which were situated at the end of the main corridors on each side, one originally for male patients and one for females.

I asked April if she ever had any issues with the hospital or any concerns with the way her mother was treated but she confirmed she had none at all. Her mother had explained to her that she was feeling a lot happier and felt incredibly safe in High Royds which eased April's concerns.

Unfortunately, despite the best efforts from numerous services such as High Royds, Norma passed away after consuming more than the recommended dose of paracetamol.

High Royds did its job in keeping her on track with her medications during her inpatients stays but may have failed to offer the correct support on discharge.

***

RHONA WADE

2000

Eve's mother, Rhona Wade, was seventy years old when she was admitted to High Royds. It was the early 2000s, which comes as a surprise since the hospital had already begun taking measures to begin its closure in the 1980s. The hospital was used on a voluntary basis to help aid her mother's recovery.

Eve's mother was battling depression before her first admittance to High Royds and was taking a tablet known as Temazepam.

Eve admitted that her mother had become addicted to the tablets which prevented her sleeping during the night and resulted in day time sleeping. Due to this, Rhona agreed to be admitted to High Royds voluntarily and was escorted via ambulance with Eve alongside. She wasn't so keen on being sent to Menston originally as she wanted to attend an ordinary hospital to begin her recovery but it seems that Eve explained to her mother the severity of the situation she was in.

Eve remembered her mother having the best humour and recalled her saying "I always wanted to live in a big house but not this one" as they made their way to High Royds.

She remembered entering through the main administration building and signing in at reception with her mother. The next steps were routine for each admission, with the individuals being escorted through the corridors which, in Rhona's case, included locked doors according to Eve. Her mother had her bags checked for any sharp objects and then handed over any medications she brought with her, which is still common practice today when you are admitted to hospital.

I asked Eve if she knew which ward her mother was admitted to during her multiple stays and she believes she was housed in both Denton and Clifton. Eve's explanation of her mother's first admittance leads me to believe that she did in fact reside here. In regards to her other stays, the tasks she did and the freedom she had, I believe that Rhona spent time on a variety of wards which I will explain further on.

Eve explained that her mother would spend most of her days staring at the walls of her ward rather that interacting with any of the other patients.

During visitation, much like other wards, families and friends would meet in the day room and were unable to enter the dormitories. I am unsure if the day room doubled as a TV room or they had a separate communal area for that. Eve did say that the TV would stay on until around nine o'clock with bedtimes beginning at seven.

Eve made an interesting observation about the beds. She insisted that the beds were placed into the walls, folded against the wall I imagine, so patients were unable to spend their days in bed. I researched into this for quite some time but was unable to find anything that matched Eve's explanation. That's not to say that Eve is incorrect, each hospital or asylum in the country had their own way of controlling patients' behaviour so this may have been a method used by High Royds, but I am unable to confirm that.

Rhona was also given ECT while she was an inpatient at High Royds Hospital which Eve explained as being a treatment option that her mother benefited from, noting that she was "perfect after."

During the summers, Eve explained that staff took their patients, including her mother, out into the gardens for the fresh air.

She also said that regular trips were organised to the local post office in Menston.

Rhona's first stay in Menston was short term, based on the average stay, lasting only ten months. On discharge, she was placed under the care of St. Mary's Hospital in Armley as an outpatient.

St. Mary's Hospital has served many purposes since it's erection in 1871-2, originally being built as a workhouse accommodating some 220 individuals. It later transformed into a maternity ward which ran until the 1970s. During the early 1990s, somewhat around 1994, the elderly was housed in Maple House, a large dwelling to the left of the administration building. If you were to stand staring at its face, it would look like a row of attached house, comprising of a main entrance which was nothing more than small glassed porch with the sign 'Maple House entrance' positioned above the double doors. Around 1996, the elderly had been relocated and patients from Ramsgill, a ward situated in High Royds, moved into the housing. The patients who resided in Maple House were not dangerous nor needed sectioning, they resided in the House as they were unable to live in the community on their own and needed assistance with washing and feeding. There was an immediate care team, or an assisted daily living service that helped the patients of Maple House. The patients were allowed to freely move about the grounds of St. Mary's and potentially only confined to their houses in the evening, with the doors being locked. It is said that there were no services in 1996 for the patients of Maple House and I am unsure if this is true, but it is confirmed that the hospital did move forward into mental health services after the maternity ward closed down. Maple House has now been demolished with staff being told that the building was not fit for purpose and repair costs were becoming too expensive. The grounds of St. Mary's still operate today, offering community health services for the elderly and inpatient opportunities for those with learning disabilities.

Rhona would attend the day centre at St. Mary's, visiting at least three days a week in the early stages after her discharge. Eve noted that her mother would gradually reduce the times she attended before being re-admitted to High Royds. Eve said her mother wanted to go back to the asylum shortly after her first discharge but eventually settled with the services offered at St. Marys. Rhona would still require appointments with her consultant regularly which would be held at St. Mary's and would be carried out every six months.

During one of Rhona's discharges from High Royds, Eve remembered her overdosing on two separate occasions, alongside having bowel cancer.

Rhona had called her daughter after taking the medication but Eve checked her over and deemed her well. It was clear to Eve, that her mother couldn't cope outside of the establishment and had gotten accustom to a daily routine.

I am unsure if this was Rhona's second admission or a further one, but I believe she was admitted to one of the rehabilitation wards at one point. Eve explained how her mother was taught to cook her own meals whilst setting their own tables. However, Rhona apparently wasn't too involved in the rehabilitation side in the beginning as she felt uncomfortable eating in front of strangers. During her first evening, Eve said that she ate her meals by her bedside which was organised by the staff. The second night, the staff would only allow Rhona to eat her meal at the end of her bed which lead to eating it in the corridor the following evening. Finally, Rhona would eat her meal in the dining area alongside other patients as the days progressed. Staff used the method to slowly coax Rhona away from her bedside and towards the dining room, small movements each evening. Eve remembered that it was the treacle sponge and custard that pulled her mother into the dining room that final evening as it was her favourite desert.

After Rhona's final discharge and with High Royds finally closing its doors on mental health, she would find herself in the care of The Mount near Hyde Park.

This small service today offers the Leeds Older People Inpatient Service which has separate wards for those with mental health needs; dementia and learning disabilities.

Eve said her mother spent a couple of months here as she enjoyed being institutionalised, preferring to have nurses on call than living independently.

After years of battling with her mental health, Rhona had finally settled in Wheatfield's Hospice due to her progressing cancer.

Sadly, in 2018, Rhona passed away at the age of eighty.

Rhona was an example of why institutions such as High Royds were excellent in aiding recovery. After leaving, Rhona struggled to settle back into independent life and preferred a setting with strict routines which ultimately left her being institutionalised. To Rhona however, this was something she enjoyed and coped with. Much like others, who were identical to Rhona, it may have been unsatisfactory to send these individuals out of an asylum life unaided.

***

PART TWO

NORWOOD HOUSE & RIGTON

The male chronic block wasn't erected during the hospital's original construction, nor was it included in the plans. The main asylum was designed to incorporate extra wards if required and that came about during the mid-1890s as two additional buildings were constructed on the outer ends of the echelon wings which brought the patient count up to 1600 from 900.

The building's design took the shape of the letter "H" and set within its walls were the wards Rigton, Lindley, Ribston and Grassington. When the institution was built, females and males were segregated however, around the 1960's the genders were allowed to mix. For those who are not aware, a chronic ward was a destination most fitting for patients whose condition would likely not see an improvement.

It is hard to paint a picture of what the inside of these walls showcased, mainly due to the fact that there are no photographs online showing the ward in motion. I can only go by the décor which remained during the change over from the lively wards to the social club which had embedded its roots on a temporary basis while its previous residence was under demolition. So, if I was to set the scene for Rigton, also for the other three wards, assuming that the décor followed suit, I will have to go on the very few photographs during final transformation into housing.

The walls were painted with two colours, burgundy and white. The colours were coated parallel to each other, with burgundy being on the upper. All rooms were equipped with cast iron radiators, glossed in a striking red which interconnected with the colour scheme. Within the main rooms and/or wards, wood panelling was used across the foot of the walls and rather than white, a more achromatic grey was given to these boards. These panels were not used in the corridors; the lower portion was simply painted in the same shade. The face of the doors, as viewed from inside the room, was painted a raisin black, with the reverse painted in a lighter tone of red. Connecting corridors were thin, not to the point where passing someone side-by-side would have been difficult, but thin enough to cause a small amount of chaos if an abundance of characters were made to file their way through at the same time. The ends were capped off with tall windows; white iron bars crossed one and other to create a secure barrier, preventing any individuals from escaping. Much smaller radiators were positioned directly beneath, painted white and fixated to the walls. Staircases were decorated in the same fashion, but the colours were reversed. Burgundy was used on the inferior portion of the wall with the white continuing on upwards to the ceiling. Standard wooden handrails were aligned along the staircase, giving that extra support for ascending and descending the stairway. Windows were located on the turns of the stairs, but these did not come paired with iron bars, only simple, 1920's style net curtains. If I were to take a guess on why this was, I would assume that the barriers were only used in and around patient quarters. I would suspect that the flooring would have been simple, linoleum style however, as seen in some images; a burgundy carpet could be seen rolled up against the wall. This could have been from the social club days as a carpet would make more sense, but I can't guarantee that.

From research and individual recollections, Rigton had three padded solitary confinement cells, or padded cells to the later generation. As High Royds was a Victorian asylum I assume that the original cells had double locking doors with the padding made from leather, then filled with horse hair and painted the desired colour. Towards the final stages of the hospital, one would guess that the padding was replaced with a more modern cushioning such as foam and plastic coverings.

Besides the individual cells, the larger spaces were filled with beds, simple, cast iron and placed within rows one after another, side by side. It is hard to say how many beds were designated to each ward but around twenty beds may have been allowed in the early stages of the hospital and more than likely downsized towards the 1960's when patient care became more of a priority.

***

If you were to venture to the far end of the asylum, past the male chronic block, you would have come across what I could only describe as a large house, not large enough to be a mansion but big enough to be somewhat in between. This dwelling sat disconnected from the main asylum, surrounded in a collection of oak trees. Inside of here, you would have found the geriatric wards, Norwood and Burnsall.

The wards were set out across two floors; Norwood was situated on the bottom with Burnsall directly above. A complete, glass-paned conservatory made up three-quarters of the face of the building which also incorporated a garden to the left.

With the villa specialising in geriatric care, patients who needed both psychiatric and medical care would find themselves residing here. As you can imagine, deaths were very common here, mostly from old age, but also from illnesses such as dementia and Alzheimer's. Depression was also common in these wards, I can only assume mainly from a death of their partners who, in those times, had relationships spanning decades. To lose someone you have spent years loving can obviously take a huge hit on your mental health.

Once inside, the décor was once again simple but more vibrant. The typical 1970s floral wallpaper showered the walls which were then met with a waterfall of lime green paint. The recurring cast iron radiators nestled perfectly under light-stained windows while the frames were lined with simple, floral curtains which conflicted with the wallpaper. Fresh air and light therapy had been used for century's, from the tuberculosis hospital in Kentucky, USA to right here in the UK at institutions such as High Royds. Doctors believed that by getting patients to sit outside and take in the fresh air and sunlight, it would improve their outcome. The use of a conservatory at Norwood clearly showed that High Royds wanted to incorporate this rehabilitation method. The use of linoleum flooring was again repeated in Norwood and Burnsall, with dark coloured flooring covering the entirety of the walkways. The large day rooms where patients would spend their time were littered with chairs and tables, walls covered in noticeboards and loose papers. The dormitories followed the same style as the rest of the home, simple décor with white concrete beams providing the room with support. Beds were simple, white and steel, placed in rows back to back and dressed with a green or blue blanket. Patients were encouraged to bring their own blankets in to make them feel more at home as most of them would unfortunately spend the remainder of their days here.

Norwood and Burnsall was a refuge, a place that held individuals who couldn't return to society and would spend their final moments amongst others who had similar fates.

***

CORA ROWNTREE

1974

Cora Rowntree fulfilled many roles during her working years within inpatient psychiatric services, at both High Royds and beyond. Her extensive recollections of her time at Menston's asylum makes for a fascinating read.

It was 1974 when Cora's journey at High Royds Hospital began. In the beginning, she received on-site training to become a Clinical Support Worker, or better known then as a Care Assistant.

Prior to her adventure in psychiatric healthcare, Cora worked as a Silver Service Waitress.

However, Cora admitted that she always had the intention to train as a nurse, originally wanting to nurse the poverty-stricken children in Africa.

Lindley Ward was Cora's destination on her first day at the hospital, which she defined as the geriatric ward for women. Originally, the block where this ward was located, alongside Rigton, was the male chronic block. Based on this development, I am unsure when the switch was made from male to female inhabitants. Cora admitted to having feelings of unease on her first day but countered them with enjoyment. She explained that morning shifts would begin at 7am, running until 2pm, where the afternoon staff would intervene and take over. Lindley is where she first encountered the male Charge Nurse for the ward, who she went on to praise.

When asked if she remembered her first day, Cora replied with "vividly." It had begun with the Charge Nurse asking Cora to help assist one of the nurses with the tea round. Cora witnessed large flasks being filled with hot water and then filled with the both milk and sugar. This prompted her to ask the question "what if they don't take sugar?" "Oh yes, they do. Most of them do. You don't have to worry about that." The nurse had replied. Cora admitted that this particular moment had stuck with her ever since.

Much like in today's hospitals, the routines are mirrored day after day and this was no different in High Royds. Cora's morning began by first waking up the patients, assisting them out of bed and helping with a bedside wash. Once a week, patients could find themselves having a bath in one of the three tubs that the ward had to offer. These baths were positioned at the centre of the bathroom and isolated from one another by curtains for privacy. Staff recorded bathing times to ensure everyone's hygiene was maintained. If patients had incontinence issues then additional baths were given. Following this, patients were helped into the wards dining area and served breakfast. With Lindley being a ward for the elderly, a majority of the patients were brought in via a wheelchair. Food, which Cora described as "wonderful," was wheeled in by local porters. I asked if Lindley had a dedicated room for feasting or if it was carried out in a multi-purpose room in which Cora agreed with the latter. Amongst the collection of patients, a nurse was assigned to a table to help feed those who needed assistance. Cora went on to explain that these allocated nurses were very attentive to the other patients, engaging in conversations, ensuring that everyone was included.

Following breakfast, patients were directed towards the lounge where they resided for the remainder of the morning, undertaking a handful of activities until lunch. The lounge, as described by Cora, housed a standard television, a radio and a collection of books and magazines. As the majority of patients had mobility issues, there weren't many intense activities planned during the times between meals, with many patients enjoying the littler things such as the radio.

While patients were occupied, the remainder of the staff would head back into the dining room and clean up. I asked if patients were made to assist with the cleaning duties but Cora confirmed they were not. She said that some patients would return and assist in ways they thought were beneficial but that usually resulted in them picking up loose crockery just to place back down moments later. Staff allowed patients to assist as it gave them a sense of purpose.

The day would continue much like it began, with patients heading off for their next meal before returning to the confines of the lounge.

Alongside general hygiene assistance, Cora and other Healthcare Assistants were allowed to carry out the changing of medical dressings. Cora remembered one patient who had acquired a serious pressure ulcer to the base of her spine.

Pressure ulcers, or sores, occur when a patient remains in the same position for a prolonged period of time. The most common areas for these sores to develop are on the areas of the skin where the bone is close to the surface. This includes the heels, spine, elbows and bottom.

The continuous pressure on Cora's patient's spine had caused a Stage 4 Pressure Ulcer. This is where the skin has broken down to an extent where the base of her spine was present through a large hole. When tending to this sore, Cora remembered having to wear two face masks. One to protect herself from the open wound, and the second, doused in perfume to mask the smell of the rotting flesh. One of the remedies that Cora carried out included stuffing the wound with bandages soaked in olive oil. When questioned about this, Cora said "Olive oil feeds the flesh so it helps it to heal. So, we were using that obviously but she was in so much pain and discomfort." Following this, the patient would be turned onto her side to relieve the pressure, alternating between each side as early as every thirty minutes. Following this, Cora took it upon herself to speak to one of the ward's doctors, which was in fact her first time interacting with one, asking them "why do we let people suffer like this." Looking at the wound, Cora said she knew that it wasn't going to heal. "Her spine started to break down and we had to massage it and when we turned her, we would massage her and everything." Patients' dressings would be changed at minimum, once a day.

Our conversation then turned on to the topic of medications. Much like other interviewees, Cora explained that medications were dispensed by the qualified nurses and would be delivered to the patients through the aid of a trolley. These trolleys also carried a large Cardex that allowed for accurate dispersion. When quizzed on the types of medications available, Cora said the most common drug she witnessed being distributed was Largactil (Chlorpromazine). At the time of Cora's tenure, Chlorpromazine had been around for only 24 years.

Alongside the use of drugs, Cora witnessed first-hand the administration of ECT and its after-effects. When asked if she knew where the ECT took place, she pointed to the direction of the Shared Services house that stood lonesome, opposite the old nursing school. Many other people who I have discussed ECT with have all explained that it was carried out in a white house, usually dubbed as the 'White House'. I can't confirm for certain whether or not the Shared Services house was home to this treatment or it was another dwelling located somewhere in the boundaries of the asylum. Cora explained that prior to the patient's appointment, they were given a tablet in order to reduce their nerves and settle them.

On one occasion, Cora escorted the patient over to the treatment centre. On arrival, she said the patient was made to wait in a small room, housing a handful of chairs. The door to the procedure room was not in fact a door, according to Cora, it was simply a curtain. Cora admitted that one occasion she had peaked through the curtain and saw the patient positioned on the table, lying flat, rubber mouth guard in place to prevent them from biting their own tongue and a brown "ear muff" instrument positioned over their temples. What Cora is referring to here are the conductors. "I didn't like it. It looked awful" she confessed. She explained that there was a nurse on either side of the patient and a doctor operating the machine. Once the machine was switched on, the patient began to convulse but as Cora recalled, it was only a slight tremor and this would have been due to the use of both anaesthetic and a muscle relaxant. After the session had finished, the patient was brought back into the small recovery room and provided a cup of tea while they settled. Cora said she would wait with the patient until they felt ready to head back to the ward. On this particular occasion, the patient was able to hold a conversation with her but not remember Cora's name. She admitted that the patient appeared shaken and dazed. Once they were escorted back to the ward, the patient was instructed to head to their bed in order to sleep off the effects.

Cora explained that it wasn't carried out as much as people believe it was, but then again, during 1974 the use of this treatment had subsided quite dramatically. She continued by saying that during her time in the hospital, it was used as a last resort; much like it is today, when all other approaches have failed.

She also had the experience of working on another of the hospital's geriatric wards, Norwood. To this day, Cora remains great friends with the Senior Sister that she worked alongside here who she described as a lovely woman.

On the topic of Norwood, she explained that it was used as a high dependency geriatric ward and some patients, who were deemed high risk, would be seated in high chairs designed for adults during meal times. Much like other geriatric wards, nurses were seated at patient's tables and helped with feeding. Residents would dine in the large conservatory that attached its self to Norwood and it was also in here that measures were taken to ensure all prepared food was suitable for the patients, with some being offered soft diets. On the subject of the conservatory, Cora explained that having this luxury made a considerable improvement to the ward's atmosphere, bringing in natural light which both staff and patients were affectionate of.

She explained that most of geriatric wards followed the same protocols so what you read here, unless stated, is information based on both wards.

Cora went on to explain that visitation was most commonly carried out in the afternoon. Much like other wards in the hospital, visitors were asked to see their friends and relatives in the dining room or other recreation room. Norwood, maybe even Lindley, allowed the visitors to see the patients at their bedside, unlike other wards. It makes sense to allow visitors to see their relatives by the bedside in geriatric wards, as many of the patients had poor mobility or were confined to their bed spaces.

When the evening came to a close, patients who were restless and immobile were assisted to their beds by the staff at around 7pm. According to Cora, there was no set bedtime so patients were free to remain in the lounge and watch the television.

On Thursday and Saturday evenings, Cora would attend the High Royds Sports and Social Club, originally situated on what is now known as High Royds Drive. She admitted to playing music in the lounge of Norwood and those patients who remained awake would be invited to dance with the staff. Many of the patients enjoyed dancing with the staff and Cora remembers one lady in particular. "One lady, Betty, I will always remember Betty, she used to say 'when are we going to dance?' And I would say 'when we get this lot to bed!'"

Moving back onto the topic of Lindley, Cora went on to explain that the ward housed a total of 42 beds, plus the addition of private side rooms.

Cora explained that due to the nature of the ward, outbreaks and disturbances were far and few. She did however recount some tales.

She first remembered a lady in which she admitted was "heart-breaking" to watch. She explained that around 4pm, the lady would begin to weep, putting herself under the impression that she had to collect her children from school. As you can imagine, the lady became frustrated, implying that the staff were preventing her from picking up her children.

The only agitation on the wards, in Cora's words, were the patients with themselves. Patients were visibly confused, wandering around aimlessly, looking for whatever they were looking for. In these scenarios, where patient agitation was heightened, Cora explained that staff would say whatever they could in order to soothe them, "to give them a bit of peace in their mind and they would go off and be happy for an hour or two, then they would be back then."

The motives for inpatients admittances have always been a topic of debate. Through the late 1800s and even earlier, women especially, could be confined to the asylum for many needless reasons. Having a baby out of wedlock was one of the common indications for an inpatient stay. I asked Cora if the patients she came into contact with during her time in High Royds were there for the correct reasons.

"They were there because, some of them was there because they were institutionalised because they had been put in at a young age and when I was on Norwood ward, one of the Sisters from upstairs, I can't remember the name of the ward from upstairs, but she had been there years and I don't know how they came onto the ward but there were these old files and she actually showed us the patients on the ward and they used to take a photograph of them and the photograph was in the file of how they were when they came in and then you were looking at this old woman and you would think 'well why are they here?' And it's like stolen, they'd stolen something or they'd had a baby and they had been in there and they were totally institutionalised but originally there wouldn't have been anything wrong with them so no, I wouldn't say they all needed to be there at all."

Cora then went on to explain that due to the institutionalisation, High Royds became the most appropriate place for them.

As the interview began to come to a close, Cora reeled off individual memories of wards and her own experiences.

She first brought up Escroft, the clinic that sat at the peak of the main drive. She explained that many nurses were under the impression that the clinic was haunted. "But yes, everyone was convinced that… And when they looked back on the records apparently, I don't know how true it was, but it was common knowledge, everybody thought it was true anyway, that someone had hung themselves on a door down there, yes."

Rigton was the next ward that Cora dived into, explaining how the routine on there was a lot more controlled and organised compared to the geriatric units. This was due to the fact that Rigton was one of the locked wards.

To Cora's knowledge, Rigton had roughly half a dozen isolation rooms. These were also known as solitary confinement. These isolation rooms had no use of padded walls, but simply just a single bed. She explained that these were used most commonly for patient safety. She recalled one patient occupying one of these rooms.

"We had one patient called Sylvia and she was in a side room and we used to go down and get her out on a morning to get a cup of tea so she would come out and we would sit on the bed with her so she could have a cigarette but me being new, I didn't know much about her. They just said 'just be careful,' which makes you nervous to start with! So, she sits next to me and she's lighting her cig and she says to me… she used to call everyone 'Saviour'. She said 'are you Irish Saviour?' And I thought 'well do I say yes or do I say no?' And I said 'well yes, my mother was' – 'oh right,' so it was alright and then all of a sudden she got to the end of her cig and she put it on the end of her tongue and swallowed it!'

Cora then went on to describe the appearance of these rooms and another one of her interactions with Sylvia.

"They were horrible. Really high ceilings, you know, and not that wide really. But I remember one morning going to let her out because they said she could be and I had got quite confident now because I had done it a few times, you know, and she tipped the potty over my head."

On the topic of patients, Cora recalled a very young girl who she encountered at Rigton, a patient she thoroughly believed was wrongfully committed.

"She came on our ward and she was only young. I felt sorry for her. I used to get her to help me make the beds and stuff, you know, just to keep her occupied really because she liked nothing better than a bit of trouble. This young girl later became friends with another of Rigton's residents, a Jamaican woman, much older than that of the young girl. She was a great big black Jamaican and she could pick two nurses up at once and I'm not exaggerating and if she didn't want her medication, she didn't have her medication. You would get her ready on a morning and by the time you had got out of the dormitory, you would look behind you and she would be stark-naked running after you. All she did was take her clothes off. But they made friends. They got to be pals and then they, we were having new windows fitted, plastic windows because they kept breaking you see and of course, the men that came to do it, the contractors, they were from outside and they loved it because she kept stripping off. I mean it wasn't the 16-year-old but she wasn't old. She was quite fit because she was never sat still. I can't remember her name but they thought it was brilliant because we had to keep running after her to put some clothes on her, you know. I remember when she was, we were all in the bathroom, well not all of us but a few of us were in the bathroom, and it was her turn for a bath and she was in the middle bath, of three, and she said 'I want that nurse to come and wash my back' and somebody said 'I'm coming' and she said 'not you, that new one.' The curtain was round weren't they and she said 'I want that new one, just that new one.' So, I went in and had to do it but I've never seen such a big lady. I mean, really."

Cora also said that one of the further isolation rooms housed a female patient who was transferred from Rampton Psychiatric Hospital.

In 1912, Rampton Criminal Lunatic Asylum was opened in Nottinghamshire as an overspill for Broadmoor Asylum. It continues to operate today under the name Rampton Secure Hospital. In August of 2002, Ian Huntley, convicted for the Soham Murders, spent two months as an inpatient before being transferred to a mainstream prison on remand after being declared fit to stand trial.

Cora admitted that she wasn't aware of the reason for this patient's transfer to High Royds but explained that her stay in Menston was short lived due to her disruptiveness. When quizzed about her length of stay, Cora confirmed roughly one month. During her four-week stay, the woman had clawed at staff's scissors, attempting to pry them away for her own use and had also attempted to end her own life. On this particular occasion, Cora was alerted by one of the woman's friends who had exited from the ward's bathroom hysterically. Cora made her way in to find the patient attempting to hang herself using one of the bed sheets. Due to her attempt at approaching the patient rather than asking for help, Cora said she received a reprimand from the ward's Sister. The last incident that appeared to end the patient's stay at the hospital came by her act of cutting her own neck with a pin. This had unfolded in her confinement room and she was immediately transported to, as it was known at the time, Wharfedale General Hospital. The incision appeared to be superficial which allowed hospital staff to insert stitches to close the wound before returning her to High Royds. Shortly after this incident, she was transported back to Rampton.

I asked Cora why the stitches weren't carried out at High Royds and she explained that there was no surgical theatre or facilities that could accommodate this at the time however; the hospital did have a surgical wing that was added in 1927 that would have been able to facilitate this. Unfortunately, I am unaware of any limitations the surgical wing had so in this particular case, in the patient's best interest, they may have been required to attend Wharfedale.

Clifton, one of the admission wards, was Cora's next topic of discussion. She explained that there was a lot of on-to-one scenarios, or as it is known today "to special." This is where one Healthcare Assistant would provide one-to-one care for a select individual. This can be done for many reasons such as if they are a high risk of absconding, at risk of self-harm, are suffering from a confused state of mind or have a DoLS (The Deprivation of Liberty Safeguards) in place, which are part of the Mental Health Capacity Act 2005. It aims to make sure that people in care homes and hospitals are looked after in a way that does not inappropriately restrict their freedom. During Cora's time at High Royds, this one-to-one would most commonly be used to monitor a patient who has attempted to, or carried out self-harm. As it was an admissions ward, Cora said that most patients were sedated in their beds and would only leave their area of comfort to use the toilet or make a drink. It was on this ward that Cora said the psychiatrists would regularly attend as they had the duty to assess patients and plan their next step, whether that be a continued stay in the asylum, preferably relocating to another ward, or a plan to discharge.

An interesting topic that Cora brought up which I unfortunately can't pinpoint its location, was the use of a time-capsule room. She explained that it was designed to be a throwback room to the 1940s, complete with radio, gramophone and records. I could imagine records such as Empress of the

Blues by Bessie Smith and Birth of the Bebop by Charlie Parker were to be found amongst the piles. The room was finished in 1940s style décor which makes me imagine floral print walls matched with monochrome curtains or wood panelling partnered with flowered curtains. Cora remembered the resident's admiration for this.

When a patient was to pass away, Cora explained that porters would be requested in order to transport the deceased to the on-site mortuary. A nurse would also be required to accompany the porters as it was here where they had to enter the patient's details into the mortuary records.

Cora's time at High Royds lasted only six years. She was due to take temporary leave as she had fallen pregnant, but this developed into a permanent exit. She planned to carry out separate shifts to her husband, who also worked at the hospital, thus allowing at least one of them to care for their daughter. "But in the end, I couldn't bear to leave her" she admitted.

I asked Cora is she regretted leaving her role at the hospital and she confessed that she did. A few years later however, she returned as a Healthcare Assistant through an agency. This later lead to more agency work, assisting those with dementia and Alzheimer sufferers at a retreat in Leeds. I asked for her thoughts on this particular care setting and she explained:

"It was a dreadful place. It was just dreadful. I mean they had nurses, they had nursing care 24/7 there and it was like, it was a new building and it was like a circular in the middle and then you had corridors going off it. But there wasn't enough staff; do you know what I mean? To cater for it."

When High Royds closed in 2003, and years prior to that, the hospital took measures to ensure patients were transferred to appropriate services around the city. Cora believed that placing these individuals in unsuitable settings was a mistake as these newly acquired services, in Cora's opinion, didn't have the correct resources to care for someone who had spent 40 years confined to the asylum.

Finally, Cora's admiration for her fellow staff members was clear, she talked of how the Charge Nurse on her first day, and throughout her years, was always happy to answer questions and guide you on the correct path. The staff she worked alongside, from healthcare's to nurses were continuously there for each other. Staff were known to stay for years, the turn over percentage was low and patients were cared for to the standards that are carried out today.

Cora encountered many wards and services during her time in High Royds and she eventually took on extended roles in nursing and management. She truly believed that the closing of these institutions caused a greater level of harm to the inhabitants as the services they were relocated to didn't have the capabilities to care for them appropriately.

***

PART THREE

LINTON HOUSE

Linton House was segregated from the main asylum to an extent where you would not have known it was partnered with High Royds. It was situated on a small lane, now known as Norwood Avenue, with the farm to the left, and the Kanner unit towards the bottom. Linton House was a refuge for the older children, roughly from around the age of twelve to seventeen. At the age of eighteen, once one became an adult, they could be placed in the main asylum. The lodging didn't have a garden, but this didn't seem to be much of a problem as there was a wealth of fields on either side.

The building was designed and built in the shape on the letter E. Three large rooms were constructed off the main corridor and were used as classrooms and recreation rooms. A two-story extension was built towards the back which was connected by a corridor built with a running of glass windows. The extension was used for the dormitories which were decked in a light purple paint. Each child potentially had their own pine wood drawers and small wardrobe, small enough to hold around five to ten items of clothing. White curtains decorated in blue patterns draped windows which hovered above brown carpets. These seemed to be welcomed change to the linoleum which dominated the main hospital.

Heading back downstairs, the corridors were laced in shades of blue and were accompanied by wooden boards that encased the lower halves of the walls. Heading to the east of the dwelling, numerous small rooms were constructed and connected by one-way mirrors and surrounded by wooden boards, the same boards that would be used in old school gymnasiums. Rooms weren't made for interrogation, more for the observation of the children during therapy sessions. Benches lined the corridors outside; the typical blue checked working men's style and were met with the recurring brown carpet. An even smaller room, designed to house one individual at a time, stood opposite and held one phone fixed to the wall. A fine line between privacy and claustrophobia.

The most memorable part of the unit was the middle day room. A single purple door sat encased in glass. The words 'Merry' painted on the left pane and 'Christmas' on the opposite. A small detailed snowman coated the final piece of glass above the entrance. On entry, the room was painted in green, a deeper colour on the bottom and a lighter shade on the top and segregated by white trims. The green theme continued as the windows were dressed in matching curtains and an identical carpet. This room seemed to have been painted numerous times as remnants of peach and blue could be founded beneath the corroded wall.

One of the other larger rooms of the main unit was used for the classroom as children were still required to continue their academics. Flooring was this time different, simple white tiles occupied the large space which were greeted by the walls, painted in light blue and accompanied by a floral trim near the ceiling.

The final area was painted a sunshine yellow and was used for what I could only assume as a second day room or even a dining area. With wooden flooring rather than carpets.

The kitchen was positioned downstairs in the basement. It included a worktop island with beautifully tiled legs, counters that ran the length of the entire room and food storage cupboards, positioned at the foot of the stairwell.

***

GLORIA ROGERS

1980

Gloria Rogers suffered abuse both at home and in High Royds. For some, the hospital was a refuge from issues at home but for Gloria, these issues continued.

Gloria had spent her childhood with her foster family, beginning at the age of four. She recalled the first couple of years in the placement as being "okay." When Gloria reached the age of six/seven, she admitted that she fell victim to abuse from her foster family but shrugged it off as "normal" for a family in the 1980s.

She admitted that the abuse didn't have an effect when it began but she did start to feel the consequences during middle school where she eventually was expelled. It had all come about after Gloria was subject to bullying which involved another pupil labelling her as a "slag" in which Gloria retaliated, lashing at her with a pair of scissors that she was holding.

Eventually, Gloria came to the realisation that she had become the school's bully. The torment she was suffering from home had gathered inside her, causing her to take out her anger on her fellow pupils. She recalled one girl in particular who she would call "concord nose," a girl that Gloria admitted taking a disliking to, explaining that "she acted like a snob and I was poor trash."

Gloria continued to target this particular girl and remembered one specific time in the playground where she ran from the opposite side of the concrete and shoved the girl off a high wall. Apparently, the girl had fallen to such an extent where her entire legs were scraped and bleeding. Fortunately for Gloria, the girl suffered no broken bones.

At this point, Gloria acknowledged that the abuse she was receiving had turned her into someone she hated, which to this day, she regrets.

She also said that because of her occasional outbursts, she would spend a lot of her school time outside the headteacher's office, completing class work.

Gloria was suspended from school for her actions.

Back at home, Gloria explained that her abrupt behaviour would continue, stealing from the local shops and constantly fighting with her foster mother. She would also take her confined anger out on her bedroom walls, banging and screaming. During these moments of rage, Gloria explained that her foster mother would refer to her as the "devil child" and that she needed "locking up."

Before her admittance to Linton House, Gloria returned back to middle school but her stay was short lived as she was informed that because of her actions, she should have been permanently excluded from the site rather than a short suspension.

Her social worker had then informed her that she had found a "naughty" adolescent school for her to continue her academics.

On the day of her admittance to Linton House, Gloria remembered waking up in the morning and having to pack an overnight bag as her foster mother had explained to her that she was being enrolled into a school that required her to stay overnight, Monday to Friday. Gloria didn't question this and willingly made her way to the car outside. When asked why she did not question the decision to send her away, she made it clear that if she did ask questions, it would result in more physical abuse. Entering the care willingly, Gloria was unaware of where she was heading.

Admittance to Linton House is a bit of a grey area. I believe that those who were housed in here, alongside the Kanner Unit, were checked in directly with the units rather than through the main administration building. In a way, these units acted like a partnership to the hospital, running alongside the care of the main establishment without being involved thus, separate health services.

On arrival at Linton House, Gloria remembered her foster mother pressing the buzzer to gain access to the unit before checking in, stating Gloria's name. During this, Gloria remembered being ushered to the dayroom while the nurses ran over some information with her foster mother. Gloria was then taken down the halls and towards her permanent place of stay, the girls' dormitory.

During Gloria's admittance, much like the other children, she would have her mental state assessed by a variety of staff but admitted that she stuck to following the rules, behaving herself and spending as much time on her own as possible. She believes this was the reason why they wouldn't assess her as she wouldn't provide them with any types of incorrect behaviour or outbursts. She believes this was the main reason for her short stay.

Gloria described the dormitory as having dark blue walls, cascading into a brilliant white which extended from the dorms into other parts of the unit. The décor of Linton House changed as frequent as the seasons, from blues and whites, to yellow and purple throughout its years of operation.

From Linton House, or maybe during one of her times in the grounds, Gloria remembered seeing the clock tower of the administration building, which was just short of 500 yards from the unit. Regardless of the house being encased in foliage and hidden in the shadows of nearby wards, such as Norwood, the clock tower could still be seen ruling the horizon.

On her first morning in the house, Gloria said she would awake around 07:30-08:00, with members of staff getting her and the other children out of bed. She recalled one instance where one of the girls refused to awake so the staff quickly "dragged her out of bed." Gloria would then have to get dressed promptly and follow the others down to the canteen for breakfast. Shortly after, the children would head to the opposite end of the unit for school.

Gloria remembered Linton House having its own classroom for the daily studies which followed a strict timetable, beginning at 09:00 and running until 15:45. She a large blackboard on one of the walls, the same blackboard that would display the weekly lesson plan as I later found out. One particular exercise she remembered carrying out was wood burning. This task involved using soldering pens to draw an image onto a piece of wood. Gloria recalled creating an image of a cat one time. The second activity she remembered taking part in was creating patterns using mosaic tiles.

Once school had finished, Gloria explained that they were allowed to spend their remaining free time, before supper, in the day room of the unit. She remembered the walls being littered with paintings that children had made during art therapy however, she explained that these were "just for show and wasn't as nice as it was made out to be." Gloria expanded, noting that the paintings on the walls were only put in place to fool visitors and family members that the house was a worthy environment to be in, when in fact, they were merely using them as a distraction from the real problems. She described the day room as having a pool table, chairs, and a fireplace on which a tape recorder sat.

When visitation took place, Gloria believed it was carried in the day room but could only recall one of the children receiving a visitor. The rest, including her, were left to tend to other parts of the unit until the visitors left. I asked her why her placement mother didn't visit and she replied with "I don't think my placement mother was bothered or would travel this far."

Activities, where possible, would also be carried out in Linton House with staff members leading the events. Gloria admitted that they didn't happen very often but on the rare occasions that they did, they would hop on a minibus. She couldn't recall where they went but I can only assume it was some local museum or seaside trip. When day trips weren't scheduled, select children were allowed to walk the grounds of the hospital for a small amount of time, with the older children allowed to walk to the local shop outside of the asylum. During Gloria's stay, I believe the onsite shop had seized in trading.

The children were required to be in bed between 20:30 and 21:00. Gloria said all the children had to take a bath however, some would object to this but the staff didn't seem too interested in forcing the wash upon them as Gloria said staff just "let them go to bed to avoid having to deal with outbursts." According to Gloria, most of the outbursts and ill behaviour would happen at night which would prevent her from getting any rest. Children would be known to run down the corridors, attempting to avoid bedtimes. When asked what the night staff would do, Gloria just remembers them staying awake, much like today's night staff, making sure the dormitories doors were open so routine checks could be carried out to ensure all of the children were asleep.

Dormitories would include around eight beds, each separated by a roughly three-foot partition. Each bedside would have access to its own small set of drawers; pine faces and encased in white plastic with wardrobes following suit. Gloria recollected a small room connected to the dorm which housed a single bed and drawer. She wasn't sure what this room was designed to be as she only remembered one girl settling in there during her stay. The only noticeable difference between the girl and the other children, including herself, was that she was slightly older. The one thing that Gloria did remember about the girl was her stuffed brown bear that when turned upside down, would make a subtle squeaky growl. During one of the days, Gloria explained that she had taken the small "noise box" from within the bear and hid it for herself. She quickly moved away from this idea as she said "something inside my head said it's wrong and I liked the girl so put it back in and put the teddy bear back for her before she realised it wasn't making noise anymore." She remembered wanting this bear but never managed to hold it, probably the reason why the memory stuck with her.

One vivid memory that Gloria continues to carry with her relates to her first few nights in Linton House. She would be laid in bed, most likely the moon being the only light source in her dormitory, the temperature low and hearing screams, cries coming from the asylum which was only a few hundred yards from her single glazed window. She described them to me as "creepy". To hear the troubling calls coming through the darkness, I can only imagine the unsettling feeling Gloria felt.

I asked Gloria how the other children in the unit seemed to her and she remembered two girls and a boy acting "normal" just like her, until they began to kick off in which they "looked a lot worse." She also remembered another young boy who used to always play "I know him so well by Elaine

Paige" which reached the top of the singles chart in 1985. Even today, the song still takes Gloria back to her days in Linton House.

When asked about clothing, Gloria said the children would wear their own in the unit.

Gloria didn't recall any incidents at the house during her time, or any unexpected deaths, which would be an incredibly rare situation. She did however, remember one of the girls who self-harmed by cutting at her legs but she was quickly taken away by the staff to be cleaned up. I asked what happened to her and Gloria recalled overhearing the staff saying the "cuts were not deep enough for hospital." Staff had then proceeded to fill in an accident report form and place her on a 24-hour suicide watch.

Behaviour, much like in the main asylum, was monitored and managed depending on the severity. Gloria explained that the staff in Linton House would use force when dealing with disobedient children which Gloria said made the kids "kick off even more." Examples of force that Gloria used was staff grabbing the children's' arms, perhaps with the idea of escorting them to another part of the unit. Children who fought off the initial advances of the staff would eventually be restrained Gloria noted. When asked about the types of restraint techniques used, she said that the staff would usually sit on you, bending your arms to immobilise you then taking you off into another room.

If children continued being abrupt and refuse to settle down, then they would be given an injection Gloria said.

If the child did in fact calm down then they would be escorted to a bench outside of the room they were taken from until they calmed down. Gloria remembered this happening to her on a couple of occasions during her stay. Prior to her being led into the corridor, she recalled the staff member who restrained her, twisting her arm to the point where she thought it was broken.

The final step in this line of punishment involved a segregated room where the children were led. Gloria explained that the children were directed into a room through double doors and were not seen or heard from for a lengthy period of time. To this day, she is unaware of what happened once lead away. Once the children returned, they were taken into their dormitories and to Gloria, seemed extremely quiet.

It's easy to let our imaginations conjure up unimaginable things when something like this occurs. It would be easy for us to say that unspeakable torture happened behind the double doors that caused the children to return silent and them initial thoughts are caused by the stigma attached to these institutions. In theory, the staff may have just given the children verbal threats in order to calm their behaviour and keep them voiceless when returning to other children, which allowed them to continue to use that room as a form of punishment when in fact it was nothing more than an empty room. Again, I can't confirm what happened behind those double doors as Gloria is the first individual who has told that story to me so at the time of writing this, the room remains a mystery.

While on the subject of rooms in Linton House, Gloria recalled the interview rooms that were positioned off the main corridor of the unit. I believe there were a few of these rooms in the house, all having one-way mirrors which allowed psychiatrists to observe the behaviour of the child in question.

The final room that Gloria remembered was one that housed a single cream chair which she described as a dentistry chair.

If a dentist was required during the week, I can only assume that the child was either taken to a dentist off site or made to visit the consultant dentist that visited the main asylum weekly.

Situated in the main part of the asylum, just of the main corridor on the male side, was the surgical wing. Resembling nothing of a wing, the centre opened in 1927 and consisted of a variety of surgical services. The wing was only small, measuring forty-foot by thirty-foot. The hallway from the main corridor into the wing resembled a chapel roof, exposed wooden beams painted in a brilliant white, which harmonized with the walls. Décor was again simple, as expected, doors being painted in shades of either blue or salmon which met walls coated in pink or Cornish cream. A darker shade of pink was used for the flooring which stretched throughout the surgical wing.

When asked about the staff in Linton House, Gloria said they would ignore the children most of the time and would only speak to the children when they displayed poor behaviour.

I moved on to asking Gloria about medications and how they were administered at Linton House but she didn't recall any tablets being handled out, only "forcefully given" during outbreaks.

Gloria did however bring up the treatment known as ear syringing. Since as long as she can remember, Gloria said she always had trouble concentrating on more than one situation at a time. During one of the many lessons held in the unit, one of the staff members made the assumption that Gloria wasn't paying attention and made the comment that she needed her ears syringing.

For those who are unaware, individuals who have an excess build-up of wax in the ears need routine appointments to have their ears cleaned with a modernised kit. Historically, metal syringes were used to pump water into the ear canal in an attempt to dislodge and flush out ear wax. Today's kits are designed to squirt streams of water at different angles against the ear canal wall to avoid causing trauma to the eardrum. The less-modernised method could cause severe trauma to the inner-ear.

Further into the day, a female member of staff took Gloria into another room and explained that she would be having her ears syringed. Gloria remembers her first question being the obvious one "is it going to hurt?" The lady replied, "It won't hurt, it's just like going underwater. We need to clean your ears."

The treatment began by the member of staff placing a small cardboard bowl beneath her ear while filling a syringe with water. She then placed the syringe into the ear and with force, pushed the stream of water into Gloria's ear canal. She then asked Gloria to tilt her head towards the bowl to allow the loose fragments of wax to fall into the bowl. As Gloria's head was tilted, she said she peered into the bowl to see the "smallest piece of wax" which is when she realised that this was more of a punishment than a treatment. When it came to flushing Gloria's second ear, she remembered the member of staff pushing down the syringe with such vigour that she felt a horrible pain strike her ear drum. To finish, Gloria was given pain relief and told to go "lie down." She continued to press the staff, insisting that her pain hadn't subsided but admits the staff didn't listen. To this day, she still suffers from issues with her right ear.

With her pending discharge becoming more of a reality, Gloria admitted that the fear of returning home had begun to sink in. The weekends she would spend back home were dreadful and the idea of returning permanently was something that Gloria wanted to avoid for as long as possible. During the evenings, she would run along the halls, creating commotion and confronting staff members. During one particular episode, Gloria explained that she entered the male dormitory and set upon one of the boys. Gloria was quickly restrained by the nearby staff and escorted back to her bedside, being monitored through the mesh windows that segregated her residence from the corridor.

Gloria continued by telling me that all the built-up anger and family secrets that she stored deep were finally beginning to surface. She realised that Linton House had become a haven for her, away from the abuse and torment, believing that if she continued to act out then the psychiatrist would have her detained for longer. As unpleasant as Linton House was, she admitted that "sometimes it still felt better than home life."

Gloria's discharge had come about at tea-time on a Friday. She remembered her placement mother having to sign some paperwork while she sat in the dayroom. Besides that, she said she didn't remember much of her departure but feels as if she would have said goodbye to the "Elaine Paige boy" who she has never heard anything from since her discharge. Her finally memory of leaving the unit was walking out of the main door, unaware if any off the staff waved her off.

Once back home in her foster placement, Gloria explained that it was "as horrible as ever." Linton House was never spoken about, nor was she asked about it by a member of the family and unfortunately, the abuse returned. She was instructed not to mention the abuse to any peers as she would end up being somewhere "much worse" as her placement mother had put it. She admitted that those words had stuck with her.

After Linton House, Gloria remembered being sent to Stonegate School which was the community's special school in Meanwood which closed its doors in 2004. The school acted as a bridge, allowing unsettled children to be weaned back into a mainstream school but unfortunately for Gloria, she remained a pupil there until she left at age sixteen.

A year later, Gloria was placed in Shadwell's Children's Home which she described as being an emergency placement.

On the day of the move, Gloria explained she was "removed" from the house after she had a row with her placement mother. During a familiar confrontation, her placement mother had hit her with a high heel which caused Gloria to, as she described it, "snap." She explained that the abuse had built up to a point where she began hitting and screaming at her in a blurred rage and admitted that she couldn't stop herself. Eventually, her placement mother had called social services and demanded that Gloria be removed from their care. As the social worker arrived at the house, Gloria became that petrified that she barricaded herself into her room and was only broken free when they finally made their way in. After she was dragged into the parked car outside, she had begun to kick at the windows. Besides the obvious reasons behind Gloria kicking at the car's windows, I asked her if there was any other reason behind her rage and she explained that her outburst was due to fear. Her foster mother had threated her with a far worse place than her home if she ever told anyone of the abuse. "I was frightened as I thought I was going somewhere to maybe die as that was worse than what I was going through at home."

Eventually, Gloria's shoes were removed eventually to prevent the windows being damaged.

The placement was indeed temporary as Gloria was transferred over to Luttrell Crescent a week later. This would not be her final settling though, as she was moved once more to Iveson Approach and remained there until she was seventeen.

Finally, she used the help of Barnardo's to find her permanent accommodation. She explained that Barnardo's helped care leavers find their own accommodation and that is correct, in 2014-15, they helped over 3000 care leavers find permanent residence.

Shockingly, in 2010, Gloria finally found out that Linton House resided within an asylum and was not the "naughty school" that her placement mother had branded it as. She had only found this out after a social worker reached out to her.

She was contacted because a case had been brought forward against her old placement family which was centred on abuse allegations. She was asked to attend a court case and give a statement in regards to the abuse she suffered during her childhood while under their care. Gloria admitted "it was hard but I did it and protected other children." It was at that point during the court case that Linton House was mentioned. She knew the unit was known as this but wasn't too sure of its actual use. The social worker for the case informed Gloria that she was housed in "Linton House Psychiatric Unit" or as it is known today, Linton House Adolescent Unit. Gloria denied this name, replying with "no, I was taken to a boarding school called Linton House because I was kicked out of middle school, and no mainstream school would take me." The social worker went onto explain that the house was used to assess the mental health state of children and young adults. Gloria unfortunately didn't go much further that this in regards to the case but I'd like to believe that those who instigated the abuse, the placement mother and her sons, were punished accordingly.

At the moment, since leaving care, Gloria still suffers from mental health issues such as depression, anxiety and has also had trouble with an eating disorder. She believes she suffers from PTSD and based on what she had been through at such a young age it comes as no surprise. Gloria never found help through a professional so she admits that life never got easier.

Gloria battled through her entire childhood, from bullies at school to her own foster placement, a place where a child should feel safe. Linton House was her refuge, whether she realised it or not. Her eventual breakdown was at a time where she was able to make decisions for herself and realise her own self-worth. Allowing her to continue her life while helping to prosecute those who deserved it.

***

SHANNON GUISE

1993

Shannon's story truly shows the impact that bullying has on an individual, which in some cases adds to further grief that they already suffer from. Shannon had to deal with abuse from an early age which eventually led her to a stay in High Royds Adolescent Unit, Linton House.

It had first begun at the age of seven. Shannon said she was bullied throughout primary school and eventually, "everything got too much" resulting in her developing an eating disorder which also coincided with suicidal thoughts. The disorder had developed in 1993; three years after the bullying began.

The disorder was met with suicidal thoughts that led her to think so little of herself. I asked her if it was the way she saw herself that lead her to the decision to attempt to take her own life and she responded with "no, I was just fed up with everything and thought it would be better it I wasn't here." She went on to explain that she gathered up some tablets from her home and swallowed them. I questioned her on what was going through her mind at that moment and she told me she was thinking "this was it, it would happen straight away, and I could just die. I just didn't want to be here anymore." As the overdose didn't immediately occur, she took herself downstairs to her mother and sat herself on her knee. She asked her mother a question in hope she wouldn't get angry. She recalled saying "If I tell you something would you promise not to tell me off?" After finding out what her daughter had done, Shannon's mother, concerned, rushed her to the Leeds General Infirmary. At this point, Shannon said her parents were "very upset as you can imagine." To prevent the tablets from causing any lasting damage, Shannon said that the staff gave her some "antidote" that made her "sick for hours" until her blood levels returned to normal.

Activated charcoal is an antidote that can be taken orally or via a feeding tube. Activated charcoal is a special form of carbon that can bind other substances on its surface (adsorption). It is used to absorb drugs in the gut so the drugs don't enter the body.

After the sickness had calmed down, Shannon remembered being transferred over to High Royds Hospital and housed in the adolescent unit. She said she was very adamant about not going. She remembered her parents being visibly upset about the situation, although she knew they "wanted to do what was best to help me get better."

When she arrived at High Royds, Shannon believes she entered the grounds to the north, via the entrance just off Bingley Road which has now been sealed off. When asked about her initial arrival at High Royds, Shannon couldn't remember anything, "I may have blanked it out" she claimed.

Her first memory of the unit was being taken into the girls' dormitory, clutching her own duvet beneath her arm as she wanted to bring it with her. When asked about her first contact with the staff, she said that they came across as very friendly. As Shannon was brought in after an attempted overdose, she was placed on suicide watch and categorised as level one, thus being on constant watch by a member of staff.

I asked Shannon if she could recall what the house looked like and what it consisted of but she could only conjure up that there was a dedicated school area for academics, a pool table and a distinct room for the canteen.

When the time came for her parents to leave, Shannon fabricated the idea that she wouldn't see her parents again which lead her to become inconsolable. After this, she had made her way up to her bedside and laid herself down.

The following morning, Shannon woke around 07:30 and made her way into the canteen for breakfast. She described the canteen as not being massive but large enough to hold around thirty children. Breakfast consisted of cereal and juice. Shannon was told she couldn't leave the canteen until she had finished. One thing that intrigued me about breakfast was the fact that after they had left the canteen, Shannon alleged that they had to "go lie on their bed and not move or go to the toilet. This was so they wouldn't lose any calories they had taken in." I researched why this might have been done but came across nothing worth noting, only the fact that moving and exercising after eating can cause nausea and stomach cramps, even the occasional hiccups. Maybe this was said to children, such as Shannon, to immobilise them and reduce chaos so early into the morning.

While the children were made to sit at their bedsides after breakfast, Shannon was watched over by a nurse due to her suicide watch status. She did however, describe the nurse who watched over her as being nice.

Shortly after, school would commence and be delivered in the dedicated school room within the unit. Shannon explained the subjects were much like the ones you attended in school, English, Maths, R.E and other core subjects.

Once school had finished, Shannon said that the rest of the day was allocated to free time in which children could spend time in the communal room, which stored the pool table, and also a single computer which resided outside in the corridor. Shannon explained that the games were played from a cassette, which leads me to believe that the unit had a Commodore C64 game system. This was a system that ran games from a cassette rather than a disk like today and was made available in 1990. Those who didn't enjoy the communal room or computer could be found in the area that Shannon dubbed as the "TV room."

As part of the children's rehabilitation, Shannon remembered therapy sessions being carried out on certain days. There were two types of therapy: group therapy and family therapy. Shannon explained that group therapy would involve the children sitting around in a circle and talking about "things", talking about their feelings and how they believe things could be improved – what they would like to happen, in relation to their health and behaviour.

Family therapy was something that Shannon didn't participate in. She told me that she never really said anything during these sessions. These types of sittings would usually involve each party, the parents and the child, voicing their concerns and views on a particular subject, ideally the subject being the reason for their stay in Linton House. They would talk through their concerns and attempt to build on a better relationship.

Shannon briefly touched on the subject of a "padded room" at Linton House. She described the room as having big cushions that you could take your anger out on, crash mats that lined the floors allowing you to "do what you wanted." The thought of a padded cell inside an adolescent unit is something that doesn't immediately make sense however; some units did have a "padded cell" in a way that was decorated with colourful padded walls and floors with a variety of foam filled shapes. The best way to picture it would be to imagine a children's' soft play area.

As Shannon's first week came to an end, the children who were allowed were sent home on weekend leave and would return Monday morning. Since Shannon was still under suicide watch, she was made to stay at High Royds the entire weekend. She described the weekends as following the same routine as the weekdays which also consisted of regular visitors from family so she wasn't left too long without visits.

A few months after Shannon's admittance, she began to show signs of improvement and eventually made it to level three. This meant that she was allowed more freedom and could accompany nurses on walks around the grounds. During one of these walks, Shannon admitted that this was the first time she had tried a cigarette. At the age of twelve, she went into the village and bought a ten pack of Lambert and Butler for ninety pence. In regards to the shop keeper serving her, she said he wasn't "too fussed about us being underage." The walks were either done around the grounds of High Royds or into the village. During one of Shannon's walks she remembered walking past a nearby unit, that was unused at this point, and displayed a "creepy mannequin in the window." I'm unsure what unit Shannon was talking about. The only nearby units that were separate from the main site would have been either the Kanner Unit, which housed babies up to the age of 10 and the infectious hospital which stood on the opposite side of the road to the Kanner Unit. Shannon's account took place in 1993 and I am unsure when these surrounding services had stopped operating.

With Shannon's condition improving significantly, she was allowed to return home for the weekend like most of the other children. Shannon said this was done so she could slowly integrate back into "normal life." However, during her returns back to the unit, she would occasionally attempt to escape and run back home to her parents. I asked Shannon if her parents were surprised when she showed up unannounced on the doorstep but she said "they knew I was coming as the unit would have called them to let them know. They would just say I have to go back as it was the best thing to do."

Shannon recalled her hate for her parents at times like that which is understandable. I asked her why she wanted to run away from Linton House and she simply told me that she just didn't want to be there. She doesn't remember how she escaped, just remembers running off. Shannon did however, remember a time when she was out in the nearby field and attempted to make a run for it, only to be wrestled to the ground by a nearby nurse. The consequences of this were that Shannon was put under a watchful eye for a few weeks until she could be trusted again. When asked if she was punished for behaviour like this, she said she wasn't really, she was just "told off."

As Shannon's stay at High Royds came to a close, her behaviour began to change, she didn't attempt to run away but actually wanted to remain there rather than go back home. She recalled feeling safe, feeling hidden away from the world which she found comfort in. Afraid to return to normal life is how she described it. With her regular visits back home for the weekend, Shannon began to settle back in. She told me she made some good friends during her stay at Linton House but was unable to stay in contact after her discharge as the unit though that it was unhealthy to do this.

Shannon couldn't remember much of how her discharge day came about, but remembered being sad that she wouldn't see any of the nurses again as she was quite fond of a few of them.

Her attendance at school began to steadily improve and there was no talk from her fellow pupils. She settled back into her home life and continued to attend regular counselling sessions to aid her recovery. The sessions weren't held at High Royds, but small group sessions held at the Leeds General Infirmary.

She continues to manage her life well; she admitted that she has the occasional "wobble" but despite everything, managed to come through everything that was thrown at her. I asked her to summarise her stay at Linton House and this is what she had to say:

"I would say it was helpful and the staff were really good, I guess if I hadn't have gone then things would have gotten worse and I might have done myself lasting damage."

I believe Shannon's stay was more aimed at monitoring her behaviour and keeping her in an environment where she could be watched rather than a stay of punishment. Like Shannon said, if she hadn't gone to Linton House, she may have done lasting damage and eventually taken her own life. The adolescent unit provided Shannon with an environment where she was able recover and rehabilitate.

***

CAITLIN EASTCOTT

1997

Caitlan Eastcott was admitted to High Royds during a time where the services were gradually being relocated into the community. She was admitted just six years prior to the closure of the hospital.

Prior to her stay, she told me she was homeless and living out of a women's refuge.

During her time there, she was prescribed Valium, an amount that she referred to as excessive. She recalls that the Valium caused her psychosis.

Valium was prescribed to those who were suffering from anxiety disorders such as OCD and panic disorders. One of the side effects of Valium is increased worsening of depression and panic attacks. Caitlan could be correct in saying that Valium worsened her condition.

She was first admitted at the age of eighteen and this was Caitlan's shorter stay of the two she encountered. She was admitted to High Royds via an ambulance and explained that it was a voluntary admittance. Much like most new attendees, Caitlan was housed on Denton Ward. Caitlan didn't speak much about this first admittance and I can only assume it was a straight forward stay. She took her medications and was discharged once improvements were shown. She did point out that once discharged; she was sent back to the refuge she came from.

Caitlan's second admittance came just a year later through the form of a breakdown.

At the age of nineteen, she was sectioned and sent to Langbar. Caitlan doesn't have much recollection of the admittance and how it came about as she recalled being on "too much medication" to know what was happening. She did however; remember that she was placed on suicide watch which involves several levels based on the condition of the patient. Caitlan describes the levels as follows;

1. Level 1: 24/7 monitoring, including toilet use, bathing and sleeping.
2. Level 2: Checked on every twenty minutes.
3. Level 3: Checked hourly.
4. Level 4: Full freedom.

When Caitlan was admitted to Langbar, she was placed on Level 1.

When I asked her to describe the surroundings of the ward she stayed on, she could only recall that they were simple, ten beds to a dorm with five on each side.

She pointed out that the reason for the lack of information was because she was "out of it due to the medication."

She didn't recall how the medication was given but does know that the ones given to her in Langbar and Denton were different to the ones given to her in the community.

In regards to her second discharge, Caitlin was able to remember it vividly due to the events that unfolded beforehand. She opened up to me about her attempted suicide in the ward bathroom.

Caitlan had been feeling anxious, more anxious than usual and felt "distant" due to the medications. She labelled the day as "worst day than usual." She could feel herself unable to carry on, to move forward and felt that she needed to do something, to carry out something that would get the attention of the staff rather than, as she describes it, "drugging her up to keep her quite." When I asked her if she had ever wanted to back out of attempting to take her own life she replied simply "never." The event happened as follows:

Caitlin walked into the bathroom and tied a shoelace to the top of the cubicle. She then placed the opposite end around her neck and was about to lock the cubicle door before she was caught by another Level 1 patient being escorted to the bathroom. The nurses attempted to wrestle her down, but she continued to fight them off until there was too many for her. She was given a sedative to relax her and the next thing she could remember was waking up, back on her bed and under the supervision of a nurse. After she had attempted it once, she said it gave her the courage to try again, she knew she had a good chance of "finishing the job."

My first response was to ask her why? She explained it was a cry for help because she was feeling as if she was being constantly "drugged up."

Based on her own experience of being discharged too early, she talked of others. She remembers one girl who had been discharged after a standoff with staff, holding a piece of broken crockery. Much like herself, a day or so after a major incident, they found themselves leaving the establishment.

After the suicide attempt, Caitlan eventually made it back onto Level 4 monitoring. It took a while, she told me, and the embarrassment she had to withstand while being watched during her toilet uses or occasional bath times was degrading.

Once her discharge date had come around, she could return home. This time, her mother had found her a space at a bedsit in Armley but not long after, Caitlan had turned to street drugs.

It was known during the early 1900s that patients were given medications to "calm and quieten their behaviour." This type of practice phased out towards the end of the century but that's not to say that Caitlan didn't suffer from this type of abuse. Yes, we knew how to treat and care for those going through a crisis but that doesn't mean that we followed the correct guidelines. Caitlan could have been seen as a "troubled" patient and given a variety of medications to keep a restraint on her behaviour.

***

PART FOUR

REHABILITATION WARDS

Despite being an institution originally built to house patients away from society, High Royds implemented numerous rehabilitation wards to the site with the aim to discharge low-risk patients.

If one were to travel up the main drive towards the administration building, then stop half way, on the left you would have come across the now demolished female convalescent villa. The lodge was designed to run like the modern-day care home, allowing those who were recovering from their illnesses to receive personalised care with the aim to return them home. It is unclear why the female villa was sectioned off from the rest of the units.

The male convalescent villa was found further up the main drive and to the left and was referred to as Arncliffe House. Within this plot of land was a small number of extra dwellings, the smallest being Arncliffe, which, in essence, was not a small residence at all as it measured roughly 100 feet in length. All of the buildings within this enclosed area were merely identical, painted entirely white, with its change of colour only coming by the vintage cast iron drainpipes and open-air porch that stretched along the front of the ground floor, all of which were painted black. Inside, based off a video by Barrie Wilkinson, the home was doused in typical 1970s style wallpaper with retro mosaic flowers that were coloured in both a Cornish cream and burgundy. This retro paper covered the upper walls of the home while the lower segments were painted in mustard yellow. The carpet had a similar pattern to the walls, large white rectangles that incorporated smaller squares; coloured in a baby blue, pantone blue and red were united onto the backdrop of flax yellow.

Standing adjacent to Arncliffe was Bedale, an outpatient clinic that continued to offer rehabilitation services after patients were discharged from the care of the hospital. Bedale was much larger than its neighbouring Arncliffe, roughly being three times the size.

These two units were only accessible via the road that ran along the west of the main hospital.

The small woodland to the right of Arncliffe branched off and segregated the two buildings from the large clinic that stood behind them, known as Escroft, the admissions hospital. Behind the admissions building was another stretch of field that originally implemented numerous shelters and gardens. The original blueprints for the clinic planned for a tennis court to be situated on the east side of the Escroft however, I am unable to confirm if this went ahead as planned.

Arncliffe House and the female convalescent villa were designed to allow patients to care for themselves with multiple staff members present at all times. Patients would be taught how to cook and clean as preparation for discharge became more of a reality once they resided in these villas.

Further to the south of the asylum were multiple villas with three still remaining today. One of the lodges still stands at the entrance to the main drive way, used today as a place of worship. These lodges would become known as Sunnyside and followed the same regime as the previous rehabilitation units but without staff members present. It would be the final test for patients before being discharged completely from inpatient care.

I believe the hospital had three self-sufficient lodges in total, with the final two being found more to the east, at the foot of High Royds Drive.

***

SANDY MORGAN

1981

Sandy Morgan oversaw the closure of High Royds Hospital and had the pleasure of working in the rehabilitation unit of the hospital, Arncliffe House. She helped those, who were on their way to discharge, be able to cook, clean and look after themselves, gaining their independence back. She worked in Arncliffe, Sunnyside and within the main institution.

Prior to beginning her qualification as an Enrolled Mental Health Nurse, Sandy was employed at Presto's in Otley. She began part-time while she was still in her final years of high school before pledging full-time after her academics had seized.

Sandy finally left Presto's when she began her training to become a qualified nurse. Sandy said she always wanted to be a general nurse, one with no specialty, but decided to train to be a psychiatric nurse alongside her general nursing after speaking to a few of the resident nurses at High Royds.

Sandy's first day at High Royds fell on the 27th April 1981, which in fact was 38 years to the date I conducted this interview. Sandy didn't recall much of her first day; she only remembered details about her four-week training that was delivered onsite.

The school of nursing was nothing more than a small unit which was sited at the top of the drive and to the right, directly opposite the female's sick infirmary block, or the block to the right of the administration building. It was only small, measuring roughly eight feet on all sides and I believe it only consisted of one floor. The school had training places for sixty Registered Mental Health Nurses (RMN) and forty-five SEN (Psychiatric MI) pupil nurses per year. It trained the vast majority of nurses who would go on to initially practice in that area. In October of 1987, the students who resided there were awarded with numerous prizes by the chairman of the management committee and the hospital's Medical Director at the time, Dr R McDonald.

Sandy described the school as being small with four tutors and one manager but loved her time spent there.

The training that Sandy undertook consisted of learning the basics about illnesses, treatments and about general workings on the wards. Basic communication, alongside verbal and none verbal, were also covered at the nursing school.

Luckily, Sandy had kept hold of her student nurse uniform from High Royds and was able to send me an image of it. Sandy wore a blue dress that was decorated with both horizontal and vertical white lines (somewhat resembling the bottom of a swimming pool decorated in small blue tiles, separated by a white filler). Besides her checked uniform, Sandy was also made to wear a white nurse's cap

Occasionally, educational trips were planned and carried out to Armley Prison, Moss Side and Park Lane. Sandy explained that the prison trips were done to allow students to analyse how these environments affected an individual's mental health. She recalled being shown to the hospital wing where prisoners were on suicide watch 24 hours a day due to attempted suicide.

In regards to Moss Side and Park Lane, Sandy noted that these were both institutions for the criminally insane however, I couldn't find anything during my research to back this claim. She also explained that students had to take up placements, through no choice of their own, at general hospitals such as Otley Hospital.

They were also educated on the treatment options that were offered at High Royds, the noticeable ones being ECT, antipsychotic medications and lithium treatment. The students were also taught about the previous treatments that were carried out in the hospital, such as insulin shock therapy and lobotomies.

Sandy did mention that lobotomies had been disused since she began her placement, but does recall one gentlemen she met who "sang its praises" saying it was the making of him however, she also met a women who had adverse effects to the treatment but she was unsure what the patient was like prior to the lobotomy.

During her time, Sandy was allocated placements in local hospitals besides High Royds, with one of them being Otley General Hospital, now known as Wharfedale Hospital. Sandy was based on the surgical ward and spent between eight and twelve weeks before sitting a small exam relevant to her placement. She also confirmed they had on-the-ward observations where they would be monitored by an assessor to see how they cared for patients and carried out their duties. During this placement, Sandy also remembered being given the opportunity to witness a post mortem.

Back at the nursing school, after her final placement, Sandy was made to take one final exam in which if they passed, they would be told where they would be based as a qualified nurse in the institution. I asked Sandy if the students could choose a ward to be permanently based on but she explained that you were never asked, just told, nor did they ask if you wanted to work at High Royds they just assumed you would and placed you on a ward with a vacancy.

Sandy was placed in Arncliffe House which she described as the hospital's rehabilitation house.

She confirmed that she thoroughly enjoyed her time in the home and recalled the nurses cooking Sunday lunch for the patients each week.

During the week, Sandy explained that the patients were taught how to cook for themselves, how to budget and how to take care of personal hygiene rather than being in a strict routine like most of the patients in the main institution. She went on to say that the patients also enjoyed their time in Arncliffe as it prepared them for discharge, for life outside of the asylum.

During her time at Arncliffe, Sandy recalled an organised fun day to raise money for the house, money that would be used to buy items for the patients and funds to take the patients on day trips and short breaks. She explained that she ventured into the local shops, attempting to receive packs of Smarties for free which would be later used for a "guess how many Smarties are in the jar" game, with punters paying a small price to guess the number and potentially win a prize. Once all of the bets had been taken, the jar would be split into two piles and counted separately in two pharmacies to ensure nobody knew the final number. "It sounds boring but every little helped" Sandy said.

Sandy also remembered setting fire to the oven two Sundays in a row while she was making the Sunday lunches. The Yorkshire puddings had set on fire both times which prompted the fire bridge to be called out on each occasion. She said she felt the firemen may have become suspicious the second time it happened.

Eventually, Arncliffe House moved its services to the end of the laundry drive, or what is now known as High Royds Drive. There were two lodges that resided at the end of the lane and this was to be known as Sunnyside. Sandy explained that these houses were more suited for the services they were offering as they resembled more of a home. Each house had small bedrooms, a single bathroom and a kitchen that included a washing machine and stove.

Further back up the laundry drive, just where the tennis courts now sit, was a single home which was known as Moorview. Sandy confirmed that this was a house that the staff could rent.

Another lodge could also be found at the foot of Guiseley Drive, which was the main driveway to the administration building and was used as part of Sunnyside services. Sandy described the lodges as self-contained homes with patients living in groups, with the aim to keep them together when they were eventually discharged back into a community setting.

I asked her what the average length of stay was in these homes as I imagine that the waiting list to transfer patients from the main hospital into the rehabilitation services was a long one. She explained that the length of stay was dependant on many factors with the main point being able to find suitable accommodation based on the individual's needs. Patients would usually stay for several months with many residing there for year.

With the service moving from the large unit known as Arncliffe House to the Sunnyside lodges, I asked Sandy what the main differences were and she noted that the unit was staffed while the lodges were not. Lodge patients would either be visited when required or Sandy said they would try visit once a day if possible, to ensure everything was okay.

Sandy went onto explain that the lodge at the bottom of the main drive housed three women during her time there and staff had to only visit once a week, not because they required it but just to carry out a general check on their wellbeing and offer any support if necessary.

I asked Sandy what a typical day working with the residents of Sunnyside included and she explained that it was fairly laid back. The staff would assist patients with daily activities such as shopping, cleaning and cooking. It is difficult to say whether these men and women were actually patients while in the lodges as the definition of a patient is "a person receiving or registered to receive medical treatment." I can only assume that the occupants were not receiving any medical care, only assistance with daily living which in that case, I wouldn't consider them as patients. I mean yes, they were under the care of High Royds but not from a medical sense, only been kept within the hospital until an appropriate accommodation became available.

I am unsure if Arncliffe House seized its services when they relocated to the lodges or if it continued to offer beginners care for those moving from the main asylum that weren't ready for discharge. As Sandy explained, the lodges were designed to replicate homes and contained no staff members but it doesn't seem like the ideal environment for someone who has just be introduced into assisted living. I believe that Arncliffe continued to offer its services as a starting position for individuals who would then make their way into the lodges before being discharged completely from the care of High Royds.

At this point in the interview, Sandy spoke about her time on Rigton, the ward she described as the rehabilitation ward, alongside Ribston. From what I understand, Rigton was found within the chronic block towards the north-west of the hospital. With that being said, I am unsure if the use of the ward changed later into the century. Sandy explained this was the place where the rehabilitation began, a ward where the patients would learn to clean their own clothes and choose their own bath times rather than relying on a set bathroom schedule.

I asked Sandy if she could run me through a typical day from start to finish and she was able to do that in great detail.

The day would begin by the day staff, including Sandy, receiving a handover from the night team. This handover would give the day staff an update on each patient and any changes that have been observed overnight. Sandy would begin by waking the patients and having them out of their beds, washed and dressed, ideally all before breakfast. Patients would then be required to attend their given therapy sessions for the day.

There may have been two locations for the therapy sessions, one being the Beamsley ward which was known as the Occupational Therapy ward and the second being the small unit that sat atop the small embankment opposite Ribston which may have been known as Harewood Therapy.

"Harewood", from the outside, resembled a school gymnasium. It measured roughly 114 feet in length and around 45 feet in width. Its small size was lost in the shadow of the chronic block which stood to its right. The therapy building was erected in brown stone which carried a white trim along the top. From above, it appears that the unit was split into four individual rooms as it had four distinct roof frames spread along the length. Sandy described the inside as being one large room, with the addition of a kitchen, cloakroom and toilets.

A local company by the name of Wendy Wools, a fabrics manufacturer in Guiseley, would send work into the asylum for patients to complete during their practical therapy sessions.

With this being a rehabilitation environment, I assume the sessions involved lots of arts and craft, cooking and other activities that they could incorporate into their daily lives once they are released from the institution.

After therapy, patients would return to the ward and take their places for lunch. The therapy sessions would continue once again after their afternoon meal before they returned to the ward for the second time to eat supper. Once into the evening, patients were allowed to watch TV in the ward's day room or take part in any of the activities that the staff organised, such as bingo or hair and makeup sessions for the ladies.

During the weekend, staff would arrange day trips to the local cinema, shopping trips, meals at Harry Ramsden's and even take the hospital's minibus to the coast.

In regards to the rehabilitation aspect of the ward, Sandy explained that patients were split into groups that were nurse led and were taught how to budget, shop for themselves and even how to catch a bus which Sandy explained that most of them had probably never done. In regards to medication, the nurses would also teach patients how to self-administer their own doses, taking note of the information printed on the box.

I asked Sandy what medications she most commonly came across during her time at High Royds and she listed me the following; thioridazine, chlorpromazine, procyclidine, carbamazepine and lithium.

Thioridazine, which presented itself as a small orange tablet, is used for the management of schizophrenic patients who fail to respond adequately to treatment with other antipsychotic drugs.

Procyclidine is used to treat symptoms of Parkinson's disease or involuntary movements due to the side effects of certain psychiatric drugs (antipsychotics such as chlorpromazine/haloperidol). It is presented as a white tablet.

Carbamazepine is an anticonvulsant. It works by decreasing nerve impulses that cause seizures and nerve pain, such as tregiminal neuralgia and diabetic neuropathy. It is also used to treat bipolar disorder. It is given in tablet form put presents itself in a variety of colours depending on the brand used.

I won't cover chlorpromazine or lithium as I have described its uses previously in this book.

Sandy also mentioned that once a month, both Rigton and Ribston would come together and hold a party. She was quick to praise the parties, explaining that both staff and patients thoroughly enjoyed the festivities with sandwiches, beer, and other refreshments on offer. There would also be music for dancing in which Sandy further explained that the nurses "were like entertainers at Butlins", attempting to entertain the masses. On the subject of alcohol, Sandy explained some patients were prescribed Guinness.

Funnily enough, doctors were known to prescribe Guinness, or recommend it, to pregnant women as it was supposedly a good source of iron and expecting mothers were required to have fifty percent more iron that they usually would have. It's hard to put a date on when doctors would have suggested this.

Sandy continued to explain that the parties that did offer alcoholic drinks had to be monitored closely by the staff to ensure those on certain medications wouldn't try sneak one from under the nurses' noses. She did however; say that those who did drink would only have a few glasses.

On Wednesday 29th July 1981, an estimated 750 million people from around the globe witnessed Prince Charles marry Lady Diana Spencer at St Paul's Cathedral in London. The staff and patients of High Royds were also to be included in that figure as Sandy recalled setting up a large TV, that one of her fellow staff members brought in, within one of the wards dayrooms. Accompanied by food and beer, the room celebrated with laughter and dancing. This wasn't the only occasion that parties such as this were organised as Sandy said "we did try to do a lot, I remember making special celebrations for birthdays, Christmas and even Easter."

During Sandy's training, she explained that she worked on most wards throughout the asylum and once qualified, she returned to take charge. To become fully qualified as a nurse, it takes roughly three years of full-time training which leads me to believe that Sandy qualified around 1984. The most common wards that she took charge on were Burnsall, Norwood, Masham, Arncliffe and Sunnyside.

Sandy recalled one shift on Rylstone in which she took charge. During the beginning of the shift, Sandy explained it was just her and an auxiliary (Healthcare Assistant) and neither of them were familiar with the ward as they had been transferred from their own wards that same morning. By the time that medication was due to be dispensed; Sandy had to contact the nursing officer as she was unaware of any of her patients' details in order to provide them. A nurse was later sent to Rylstone to help assist but her stay was short as she trapped her finger in one of the fire exits as she attempted to prop it open and required medical attention. Sandy was then left to contact the ward Sister from the ward below and thankfully, she was also trained in general and psychiatric nursing so was able to offer her services. Due to the fact that Sandy was left on her own until the Sister arrived, I asked her how she felt about that and she described the ward as an easy environment which makes me believe that she coped just fine on her own.

Sandy also noted that she was also the vice chairwoman of the High Royds Social Club.

In 1984, Sandy completed her training and became an Enrolled Nurse, later undertaking further training to become a Registered Nurse in 1994.

In January 1986, Sandy closed the chapter on High Royds and moved down south with her partner. It was her partners idea to move away and Sandy was happy to follow as she believed moving into new nursing environments would have been an excellent experience. During her time in the south, Sandy continued to nurse and found herself working for Exminister Hospital.

Exminister Hospital was also a mental health facility that opened in July 1845. It was built as a military hospital during the First World War and later became the Devon Mental Hospital in the 1920s. The movement to Care in the Community affected the hospital, much like most asylums around the country, and it closed in July 1985.

Sandy was there to see the closure of the hospital and was quickly transferred to work in Torbay District Hospital.

She said she enjoyed her time working down south, especially working with the elderly but the constant rush of tourists was something that Sandy couldn't work with. Ultimately, she admitted that she missed High Royds and the countryside which lead her to call her nursing officer from Menston who instructed her to return Monday morning and resume her duties as normal. Sandy expressed her gratitude for her officer for allowing her to return.

Her return to High Royds came in December 1986 and Sandy was placed to work on the Grassington ward.

Sandy explained her love for Grassington, noting that the caring staff made all the difference. She recalled one memory, where a trip to Coniston in Cumbria was organised for the weekend. She explained that Grassington held male patients only, long stay individuals who suffered mostly from psychosis, schizophrenia and bipolar. One memory of her time there involved a male patient who she recalled would pull up a chair in the corridor and stare at the wall. Sandy explained that if you were to approach the gentleman, he would describe the football match he was watching.

I am unsure if they are related however, roughly fifteen miles from High Royds was another hospital, Grassington Hospital. In 1919, the Bradford Health Authority had purchased a collection of meadows alongside Hebden Road which would later become the home of Grassington Hospital. The idea was to construct a sanatorium that would house and treat patients suffering from Tuberculosis (TB.) The main building of the establishment was designed so that the rooms would open out onto a large balcony and allow patients to breath in the Dales fresh air. Patients would be sent here in the hope that the fresh air would help them recover from TB. Around the 1920s, the Bacillus Calmette-Guérin vaccine, also known as BCG, was introduced to treat those suffering from TB. Due to this, the hospital began to decline which forced a change in services, ceasing as a sanatorium in 1966 and transitioning into a Psycho-Geriatric hospital which played as an extension to High Royds. The doors of the hospital finally closed in 1984. With the hospital acting as an annex to High Royds, I am unsure if when they renamed the wards in the 1960s, that they chose to name one of them Grassington after the former TB hospital, or it was simply named after a town in North Yorkshire, much like the remaining wards named after nearby towns.

Shortly after, Sandy was relocated to Chevin Day Hospital as she had recently become a single mother of two children and required a Monday to Friday role.

Chevin Day Hospital was positioned to the rear of the site, down the corridor from Hebden House.

Sandy explained that the day hospital was an outpatient environment that supplied activities for those visiting. She described it as a great place for returning patients who would indulge in crafts, quizzes, improve their social skills and get help for any problems that arose at home. The service also allowed patients to speak to a doctor if they had any concerns and organise their medications. The service also allowed some patients to have an assisted bath and have their hair washed. Sandy also explained that if patients visited around lunch then they would be greeted with a hot meal.

Eventually, with High Royds beginning to relocate its services, Sandy explained that Chevin Day Hospital was moved over to St. Mary's Hospital, Armley in 1992. This service operated differently to Maple House as the outpatient's clinic remained as an outpatient service with patients being picked up from their residence via minibus and brought to St. Marys for the day, before being taken back home. Sandy followed with the service and explained that the daily duties remained and followed the same patterns as Chevin Day Hospital. I asked Sandy why it was moved so early, roughly eleven years prior to the asylums closure, and she explained that the closure of the hospital was on the cards since she began in 1981, which she believed was why the hospital began to offer multiple rehabilitation services, a way to prepare them for discharge rather than transfer them to other struggling services. Sandy remained with the outpatient clinic for roughly four years before returning to High Royds.

On Sandy's final return to High Royds, she returned to the rehabilitation services and worked adjacent to the old Arncliffe House, residing in Bedale.

Bedale resided on the same drive as the Escroft Clinic but was not accessible through the same road, with the entrance to Bedale joining from the lane that ran up to the Beamsley Block. During Sandy's time, it acted as both an outpatient's clinic and therapy block. It was built larger than the neighbouring Arncliffe House, being roughly three times the size.

Sandy described it as an acute day hospital where patients would make their own way to the unit and make their own way home. It acted similar to Chevin Day Hospital, a doctor on hand to discuss any concerns and staff could monitor any signs of change in the individual's health. The service also offered one-to-one time with nurses so they could discuss any issues they had at home and make any suggestions and recommendations. The unit would also dispense any medications that the patients needed on a weekly basis and administer long term injections to control any symptoms. Much like Grassington and Chevin, Sandy described the staff as being caring and always offering suggestions to better the service.

In November 1996, the service was moved into the community in Yeadon which closed the chapter for the final time for Sandy, bringing to an end a ten-year career at the hospital.

She described this service as being a reflection of Bedale but more developed in the services it offered such as more one-to-one support.

I asked Sandy how the atmosphere was before her departure and she explained that it was mixed. The staff, including her, were glad that the services for mental health were improving and that individuals suffering these mental illnesses wouldn't be confined to a hospital for the remainder of their lives and cared for more in the community. On the other hand, Sandy also explained that institutions such as High Royds were a haven for some and recalled a patient at the time telling her that if he was made to leave the hospital then he would proceed to steal a pork pie in order to be readmitted as he was under the impression that this was the reason for his admission.

Sandy also said, "Imagine a village being emptied and how eerie that would be."

She went on to describe how she loved every minute that she worked at High Royds, insisting that if there was abuse present in the asylum and lack of patient care, she would have left and carried out general nursing elsewhere.

Sandy worked at the hospital during a time where the NHS had control over the care given, in which we would all like to think that acts of abuse had been stamped out by the service. That is not to say that the abuse stopped completely as we all know that even today, abuse is still present in many healthcare settings. Sandy clearly surrounded herself with a team of staff that knew how to care and provide services that patients benefited from which, in due course, led to their final discharge.

She also spoke about the period where the day hospital at Yeadon was later transferred over to another service on Hyde Terrace in Leeds. The patients had gone ahead and campaigned about the move and Sandy recalled it being spoken about in the House of Commons. They campaigned because they were against the proposed move however; their pleas were unheard as the service eventually moved to Hyde Terrace.

Sandy continued her role in service in Yeadon until 2016.

Sandy saw asylums in a different light of those before her as she witnessed the fall of the Victorian institutions. High Royds was sensible towards its final few years, choosing to rehabilitate inpatients, preparing them for life outside of the hospital, rather than shipping them off to other inpatient facilities. To some, this may have been the most appropriate method, but for those who had been institutionalised, life outside of a strict routine will have come as a surprise. Despite the reasons behind the opening of the asylum, High Royds closed its doors by helping those in its care find the most fitting environment.

***

SUMMARY

As of writing this conclusion, the doors of High Royds Hospital have been closed for seventeen years.

It is clear that from these stories that High Royds offered both exceptional and dishonest care to thousands of its patients who were fortunate and unfortunate to reside within its walls.

We conjured up an idea to house these "idiots" in institutions that were constructed away from the public eye, with the aim, in the beginning, to simply remove them from society.

This is evidential in the early years of High Royds as many of the deceased, who were buried in Buckle Lane cemetery, never had their remains collected or identified by their families.

When we did begin to "treat" mental illness, we used inhumane procedures such as the Lobotomy.

Rather the treating the psychological issues with these individuals, doctors would merely use methods to minimize physical outbreaks, controlling behavior rather looking at the root cause.

In today's society, we continue to treat those suffering from mental illness with a variety of options such as therapy and medications. Antipsychotics, antidepressants and mild sedatives are the most common medications used however; ECT is still used if all other options fail.

Today's Electroconvulsive Therapy is a far more advanced version that what was used in Victorian asylums. Patients are rendered unconscious through a general anesthetic and given multiple sessions under strict guidelines.

Despite the closure of the asylums, many of the old institutions still operate today, providing inpatient psychiatric care to vulnerable individuals. A lot of us are under the impression that every asylum seized its services and were either transformed into housing communities, demolished or left for nature to reclaim.

Take Hellesdon Hospital in Norfolk for example which opened as the Norwich Pauper Asylum in 1828 before being rebuilt in 1880 as the Norwich Borough Asylum. It gained multiple extensions during the 20th century and was renamed as the Norwich City Mental Hospital in the 1920s before joining the NHS as Hellesdon Hospital in 1948. Despite modern facilities being added to the rear of the hospital, the main accommodation remains in use.

Rather than large institutions, smaller, more modern units are being used to treat those suffering from mental health conditions with the Becklin Centre at St. James Hospital being a prime example. The service opened in 2002 with the aim to house multiple patients from High Royds Hospital.

We birthed the idea of asylums as a refuge for suffering individuals but failed to provide a rehabilitation side in the early years, relying on deaths to allow new patients to enter the asylum system. As the years progressed and medications began to channel their way into institutions, asylums around the country began to become outdated and unnecessary. It is easy to point the finger at these establishments as places of cruelty and neglect but the truth is, without the hospitals, we may be further behind in the care of those suffering with mental health issues than we are today.

In the final pages, you will read an interview with Laura Turner. A Student Nurse who had the chance to work in a modern ECT Clinic.

***

LAURA TURNER

2019

From the beginning, I have always envisioned concluding this book by interviewing an individual who currently works within a modern mental health setting and Laura Turner approached me to offer her personal insight into the psychiatric world.

Laura's personal connection to High Royds comes by the way of her grandmother who worked at the hospital. It is from her, that Laura was educated about the asylum. Laura spent her adolescent years residing in Tranmere Park Estate, a neighborhood situated just off Bradford Road. As a child, she did venture into the grounds of the asylum to sledge during the winter periods and came into contact with absconding patients towards the hospital's boundaries.

Laura admitted that she has always had a fascination with people and the psychology behind what makes us all unique. This fondness drove her to study psychology and eventually, due to her enjoyment of the topic, lead her to commence a nursing degree.

Prior to achieving her Master's Degree in Mental Health Nursing, Laura undertook paid work at an inpatient eating disorder service for a total of two years. She also gained experience working with individuals who suffered with moderate to severe disabilities, offering her services to the local charity, Airborough Supported Activity Scheme at the young age of fifteen. This charity aimed to support children between the ages of four and nineteen.

To support her ongoing nursing studies, Laura worked at various mental health and elderly support services.

"I just knew I wanted to work with people and try to ensure those who have an unfair disadvantage in life, can experience things in the best possible way and to have a good quality of life. I've had personal experiences with mental health and supported friends and family with the same. Knowing the value of mental health services and the sheer lack of them made me want to help I suppose."

The Hadrian Clinic in Newcastle is a Physical Treatment Centre that offers ECT, a Depot Clinic and a Clozapine Clinic.

A Depot Clinic is a service that offers depot injections. This type of injection offers a slow-release form of the patient's typical antipsychotic. It is given in a carrier liquid that releases the medication at a much slower rate, thus remaining in the host for a much lengthier period of time.

A Clozapine Clinic aims to ensure that all users of clozapine are managed and observed in a suitable manner. Clozapine is mainly used to treat schizophrenia that has not improved following the use of other antipsychotic medicine.

It was at this clinic, during one of Laura's placements, that she witnessed Electroconvulsive Therapy. She admitted that it was fascinating to observe and had previously studied the history of the procedure during her psychology degree.

"Considering we aren't really sure exactly how it works on a neurological level, and after its portrayal in films, it has quite a stigma attached. To see it in action and the frankly phenomenal progress of the patient's presentation was astounding. Nowadays, the patient will have to have severe depression or treatment resistant schizophrenia to be considered for ECT. It's very much a last line treatment option, generally not offered to younger patients, never children. It requires consent from two separate psychiatrists. Patients are often detained under Section Three of the Mental Health Act, meaning their treatment can be enforced without their consent. This sounds a lot worse than it is in reality. I have worked with many patients under these circumstances and it is a life-saving precaution. When all of the above is in place, the nurses and the psychiatrist will develop a care plan for the treatment. Usually this is 6-8 sessions over several weeks. This can be bilateral or unilateral (electrodes are placed on one temple and top of the head, or both temples respectively). Patients are closely monitored in person. Regular nursing contact, assessment and physical observations (blood pressure, oxygen saturation, heart rate, temperate and responsiveness) are carried out for an agreed time afterwards. Patients also must have been cleared to be healthy enough so the treatment is safe for them to undergo. In clinic, patients enter, are greeted and asked a series of orientation questions (day, location etc.) All being well, patients have their physical observations taken and are briefed on the procedure. The anesthetist will give the patient a sedative and a muscle relaxant (this is to stop the muscles causing damage during a seizure.) Once unconscious, the patient has a mouth guard inserted to stop them biting their tongue or damaging their teeth. They are also ventilated to support their airways whilst under anesthesia. The area is lubricated and then the electrodes are applied that pass 70-120 volts of electricity. This is for up to 6 seconds depending on treatment prescription. The patient will usually seize but due to the relaxant this is only objectively noticeable by the face and toes. After the treatment, the patient is wheeled in the bed through to recovery where they are monitored by mental health nurses until they come around and feel well enough to return to the ward or home."

Laura explained that she was astounded of how "medical" the procedure came across, with full use of a surgical theatre and medically trained staff. She said she was perplexed of how quick the procedure was, with patients leaving the clinic as little as ninety-minutes after their initial greeting.

I asked her what her first thoughts were when she witnessed the procedure for the first time and she explained that the sight of the patient seizing took her by surprise. 'It's always strange to see people unconscious, but to see the body react physically to what we are doing is still bizarre."

"I have to say, I saw a patient barely responsive to communication in week one, to asking how I was in week six due to this treatment. Also, a fairly elderly lady at sixty-something whose depression was so severe she had stopped eating. Not only was this safe for someone her age, she improved enough at least to eat during my time there."

This encouraged me to ask Laura her opinion on the therapy and whether she believes, under the correct circumstances, that this type of treatment is beneficial. She responded with the following,

"Without making a blanket statement, I would say in the right circumstances, ECT can cause radical improvement. Like many pharmaceutical psychiatric treatments, though it has side effects such as memory loss, I think it suffers an unfair stigmatism and therefore it is easily criticized. I do think it is a treatment than can really help individuals who have often endured years of mental health illness and internal torment."

Due to Laura's study in psychology, which will have covered the history of institutions such as High Royds, I asked for her opinion on the asylum model. She answered with:

"The societal attitude towards people with mental health conditions or disability in those days was also very backwards still. Also, in isolated environments, it is easy for negative ward culture to develop and that can cause acceptability of malpractice or mistreatment. Without awareness, education, decent funding, staffing, management and hiring the right people in the first place, things that happened in those asylums could happen today to some extent."

We then got onto the topic of isolation rooms and the use of seclusion to aid one's recovery. I mentioned to Laura that High Royds had its fair share of these and explained to her, much like I did in the scene setting for the Beamsley Block, the layout of the asylum's confinement rooms. She went on to explain how they are used in today's modern settings.

"These are empty rooms with nothing in that a patient could use to injure themselves or others. In order to pass food and care for them, planned restraints are used to safely do so. This can take up to five members of trained staff. This is done with as much cooperation as possible and the patients are monitored throughout. Some patients request seclusion because they find the outside world too overwhelming when they are unwell. They can have music, talk and play games through the windows with staff so they are not void of stimulation should they wish it."

I then went on to ask Laura if she could explain the restraint process for when a patient requires to be controlled.

"They're done as therapeutically as possible. The patient is communicated with throughout and briefed afterwards. Sometimes the patient may try to grab staff or get out. However, should a patient with psychosis for example, genuinely believe the staff or fellow patients are trying to kill them, then this can be very dangerous should they choose to act on this delusion. Restraints involve the patient sat down if possible and placed in arm holds while other staff carry out tasks such as cleaning the room, giving medication or giving food and drinks. The exit is planned in a way to ensure the safety of the staff."

At the time of this interview, Laura is currently employed with a forensic service. This is an inpatient facility for those who have committed crimes and have a diagnosed mental illness. Rather than residing in a prison, they remain detained here as they require on-going medical treatment. These types of services offer locked wards and restrict patients leaving as many of them are serving substantial sentences. Laura further explained that the UK has several secure units, ranging from low to high. She confirmed that Broadmoor and Rampton are two of three high secure units and I found the third one to be Ashworth Hospital in Parkbourn, Liverpool. She was unable to confirm what service she worked at as many patients in her care have been reported in the media for the crimes they have committed.

I concluded by asking Laura what the future holds for her and she told me:

"Well I'll qualify in February 2020 and find something back home, hopefully in forensics or potentially eating disorders. I hope to do another postgraduate in therapy and pursue a nurse therapist career. As long as I'm working with people and the NHS doesn't implode all should be well. I've had a nightmare funding the course, I wrote to my MP and plan to do an article at some point about it. Considering how desperate they are for us, they make it very, very difficult to get there."

It was fascinating to talk with Laura and get a first-hand account of modern day ECT and the workings of today's psychiatric inpatient services. I wish her the greatest of luck in her approaching career.

***

REFERENCES

Wikipedia 2019, *High Royds Hospital*, Wikipedia, viewed on 27 November 2019,

<https://en.wikipedia.org/wiki/High_Royds_Hospital>

County Asylums n.d., *High Royds,* County Asylums, viewed on 27 November 2019,

<https://www.countyasylums.co.uk/high-royds-menston/>

The National Archives, *High Royds Hospital, Ilkley,* The National Archives, viewed on 27 November 2019,

<http://www.nationalarchives.gov.uk/hospitalrecords/details.asp?id=2272>

Wikipedia 2019, *Nightingale ward,* Wikipedia, viewed on 27 November 2019,

<https://en.wikipedia.org/wiki/Nightingale_ward>

Asylums Project 2016, *History of Bloodletting,* Asylums Project, viewed on 25 November 2019,

<https://asylumsprojects.wordpress.com/2016/08/26/bloodletting-history/>

Canton Asylum for Insane Indians 2014, *All in the blood,* Canton Asylum for Insane Indians, viewed on 25 November 2019,

<http://cantonasylumforinsaneindians.com/history_blog/all-in-the-blood/#more-6401>

Freyaclijmans 2012, *Gyrating Chair,* Freyaclijmans, viewed on 25 November 2019,

<https://freyaclijmans.wordpress.com/2012/11/18/gyrating-chair/>

American Asylums n.d., *Treatments Used for Insanity,* American Asylums, viewed on 25 November 2019,

<https://americanasylums.weebly.com/treatments.html>

The Time Chamber 2017, *The Asylums List,* The Time Chamber, viewed on 25 November 2019,

<https://thetimechamber.co.uk/beta/sites/asylums/asylum-history/the-asylums-list>

Western Libraries n.d., *Hydrotherapy,* Western Libraries, viewed on 25 November 2019,

<https://www.lib.uwo.ca/archives/virtualexhibits/londonasylum/hydrotherapy.html>

BCHADDA 2015, *Hydrotherapy,* BCHADDA, viewed on 25 November 2019,

<https://biancajchadda.wordpress.com/2015/02/03/ahs-asylum-truths-1-hydrotherapy/>

Drugs.com n.d., *Insulin Regular,* Drugs.com, viewed on 25 November 2019,

<https://www.drugs.com/insulin.html>

Hess-Fischl A 2019, *What is insulin?,* endocrineweb, viewed on 25 November 2019,

<https://www.endocrineweb.com/conditions/type-1-diabetes/what-insulin>

Wikipedia 2019, *Insulin Shock Therapy,* Wikipedia, viewed on 25 November 2019,

<https://en.wikipedia.org/wiki/Insulin_shock_therapy>

Columbia Law School n.d., *The History of Shock Therapy,* Columbia Law School, viewed on 25 November 2019,

<http://library.law.columbia.edu/urlmirror/CJAL/14CJAL1/shock_i.htm>

Good Therapy 2019, *Prefrontal Cortex,* Good Therapy, viewed on 25 November 2019,

<https://www.goodtherapy.org/blog/psychpedia/prefrontal-cortex>

Wikipedia 2019, *Lobotomy,* Wikipedia, viewed on 25 November 2019,

<https://en.wikipedia.org/wiki/Lobotomy>

Lewis T 2014, *Lobotomy,* Live Science, viewed on 25 November 2019,

<https://www.livescience.com/42199-lobotomy-definition.html>

Tartakovsky M 2019, *The Surprising History,* PsychCentral, viewed on 25 November 2019,

<https://psychcentral.com/blog/the-surprising-history-of-the-lobotomy/>

CCHR n.d., *History of ECT,* CCHR, viewed on 25 November 2019,

<http://www.cchr.org.uk/campaigns-overview/electro-shock-treatment/history-of-ect/>

Semkovska M 2016, *Unilateral ECT,* Healio, viewed on 25 November 2019,

<https://www.healio.com/psychiatry/depression/news/online/%7B9ba64a18-ffa5-4f7f-b032-5752f7a8a87b%7D/unilateral-ect-comparable-to-bilateral-ect-for-depression-lesser-cognitive-adverse-effects>

Hauser J 2018, *What to expect,* PsychCentral, viewed on 25 November 2019,

<https://psychcentral.com/lib/what-to-expect-from-an-electroconvulsive-therapy-ect-treatment/>

Wikipedia 2019, *Electroconvulsive Therapy,* Wikipedia, viewed on 25 November 2019,

<https://en.wikipedia.org/wiki/Electroconvulsive_therapy#History>

Wikipedia 2019, *Psychiatric medication,* Wikipedia, viewed on 25 November 2019,

<https://en.wikipedia.org/wiki/Psychiatric_medication#History>

Marston H 2013, *A Brief History,* BAP, viewed on 25 November 2019,

<https://www.bap.org.uk/articles/a-brief-history-of-psychiatric-drug-development/>

Wikipedia 2019, *Lithium,* Wikipedia, viewed on 25 November 2019,

<https://en.wikipedia.org/wiki/Lithium_(medication)#Medical_uses>

CPD 2019, *Lithium for Bipolar Disorder,* CPD, viewed on 25 November 2019,

<http://www.psychiatrycpd.co.uk/default.aspx?page=28877>

Purse M 2019, *The Discovery and History,* VeryWellMind, viewed on 25 November 2019,

<https://www.verywellmind.com/lithium-the-first-mood-stabilizer-p3-380277>

University of Leeds 2012, *Dr Roy Hullin,* University of Leeds, viewed on 25 November 2019,

> <https://www.leeds.ac.uk/forstaff/news/article/3206/dr_roy_hullin>

University of Leeds 2012, *Dr Roy P Hullin,* University of Leeds, viewed on 25 November 2019,

> <https://www.leeds.ac.uk/secretariat/obituaries/2012/hullin_roy.html>

Encyclopedia Britannica n.d., *Chlorpromazine,* Encyclopedia Britannica, viewed on 25 November 2019,

> <https://www.britannica.com/science/chlorpromazine>

Psychiatry Podcast 2018, *The History and Use of Antipsychotics,* Psychiatry Podcast, viewed on 25 November 2019,

> <https://psychiatrypodcast.com/psychiatry-psychotherapy-podcast/antipsychotics-history-use-schizophrenia>

Brought to Life n.d., *Trephination,* Brought to Life, viewed on 25 November 2019,

> <http://broughttolife.sciencemuseum.org.uk/broughttolife/techniques/trephination>

Biehal N, Parry E 2010, *Maltreatment and Allegations,* University of York, viewed on 29 August 2019,

> <https://www.york.ac.uk/inst/spru/research/pdf/FCabuse.pdf>

Anderberg J 2015, *A Beginner's Guide to Pyrography,* AOM, viewed on 29 August 2019,

> <https://www.artofmanliness.com/articles/a-beginners-guide-to-pyrography-aka-woodburning/>

Wikipedia 2019, *I Knew Him So Well*, Wikipedia, viewed on 29 August 2019,

<https://en.wikipedia.org/wiki/I_Know_Him_So_Well>

WebMD n.d., *Lithium for Dipolar Disorder*, WebMD, viewed on 06 August 2019,

<https://www.webmd.com/bipolar-disorder/guide/bipolar-disorder-lithium#1>

Wikipedia 2019, *Imipramine*, Wikipedia, viewed on 06 August 2019,

<https://en.wikipedia.org/wiki/Imipramine>

Psychiatric Disorders 2014, *History of Bipolar Disorder*, Psychiatric Disorders, viewed on 06 August 2019,

<http://psychiatric-disorders.com/bipolar-disorder/history-of-bipolar-disorder/>

NHS n.d., *Ashworth high secure hospital*, NHS, viewed on 05 December 2019,

<https://merseycare.nhs.uk/our-services/a-z-of-services/ashworth-high-secure-hospital/>

CNTW n.d., *Hadrian Clinic*, CNTW, viewed on 05 December 2019,

<https://www.cntw.nhs.uk/services/hadrian-clinic-physical-treatment-centre-ect-depot-clinic-clozapine-clinic-newcastle/>

NHS n.d., *Clozapine Clinic*, NHS, viewed on 05 December 2019,

<https://www.westlondon.nhs.uk/service/clozapine-clinic/>

Mind 2016, *What's a depot injection?*, Mind, viewed on 05 September 2019,

<https://www.mind.org.uk/information-support/drugs-and-treatments/antipsychotics/depot-injections/#.Xelkouj7TIU>

Szalavitz M 2011, *Reality Check*, Time.com, viewed 03 July 2019,

<http://healthland.time.com/2011/10/05/reality-check-why-some-brains-cant-tell-real-from-imagined/>

Wikipedia 2019, *Imipramine*, Wikipedia, viewed on 03 July 2019,

<https://en.wikipedia.org/wiki/Imipramine>

News Medical n.d., *Largactil*, News Medical, viewed on 03 July 2019,

<https://www.news-medical.net/drugs/Largactil.aspx>

EMC 2015, *Modecate Concentrate Injection*, EMC, viewed on 03 July 2019,

<https://www.medicines.org.uk/emc/product/1456>

Wikipedia 2019, *Presto*, Wikipedia, viewed on 04 September 2019,

<https://en.wikipedia.org/wiki/Presto_(UK_supermarket)>

Wharfedale Observer 2012, *Nurses Given High Royds Hospital Prizes*, Wharfedale Observer, viewed on 04 September 2019,

<https://www.wharfedaleobserver.co.uk/features/featuresnostalgia/10129480.nurses-given-high-royds-hospital-prizes/>

School of Nursing n.d., *High Royds Hospital School of Nursing Yorkshire*, School of Nursing, viewed on 04 September 2019,

<http://www.schoolsofnursing.co.uk/HighRoydsHL74.htm>

Vocabulary.com n.d., *Lobotomy*, Vocabuary.com, viewed on 04 September 2019,

<https://www.vocabulary.com/dictionary/lobotomy>

Govan F 2011, *Lobotomy,* Telegraph, viewed on 04 September 2019,

<https://www.telegraph.co.uk/news/worldnews/southamerica/argentina/8679929/Lobotomy-A-history-of-the-controversial-procedure.html>

Wilkinson B 2016, *High Royds Hospital,* YouTube, viewed on 07 September 2019,

<https://www.youtube.com/watch?v=XO5J2WYK6qs>

Wilkinson B 2014, *High Royds Hospital,* YouTube, viewed on 07 September 2019,

<https://www.youtube.com/watch?v=dlsHPlknCU8>

Pastor K 2018, *Why did doctors prescribe Guinness,* Medium, viewed on 07 September 2019,

<https://medium.com/@kapastor/why-did-doctors-prescribe-guinness-to-pregnant-women-77d3fc883a>

Wikipedia 2019, *Wedding of Prince Charles and Lady Diana Spencer,* Wikipedia, viewed on 07 September 2019,

<https://en.wikipedia.org/wiki/Wedding_of_Prince_Charles_and_Lady_Diana_Spencer>

Drugs.com n.d., *Thioridazine,* Drugs.com, viewed on 07 September 2019,

<https://www.drugs.com/pro/thioridazine.html>

Drugs.com n.d., *What is chlorpromazine?,* Drugs.com, viewed on 07 September 2019,

<https://www.drugs.com/pro/thioridazine.html>

WebMD n.d., *Procyclidine,* WebMD, viewed on 07 September 2019,

> <https://www.webmd.com/drugs/2/drug-14104/procyclidine-oral/details>

Drugs.com n.d., *What is carbamazepine?,* Drugs.com, viewed on 07 September 2019,

> <https://www.drugs.com/carbamazepine.html>

Wikipedia 2019, *Exminister Hospital,* Wikipedia, viewed on 11 September 2019

> <https://en.wikipedia.org/wiki/Exminster_Hospital>

Dutta S 2019, *History of Tuberculosis,* News Medical, viewed on 11 September 2019,

> <https://www.news-medical.net/health/History-of-Tuberculosis.aspx>

Out of Oblivion n.d., *Grassington Hospital,* Out of Oblivion, viewed on 11 September 2019,

> <http://www.outofoblivion.org.uk/record.asp?id=251>

NHS n.d., *Your 6-week postnatal check,* NHS, viewed on 11 October 2019,

> <https://www.nhs.uk/conditions/pregnancy-and-baby/postnatal-check/>

Leodis n.d., *Visit to Leeds Maternity Hospital,* Leodis, viewed on 11 October 2019,

> <http://www.leodis.net/display.aspx?resourceIdentifier=2003716_19059390&DISPLAY=FULL>

NHS n.d., *Postpartum psychosis,* NHS, viewed on 11 October 2019,

> < https://www.nhs.uk/conditions/post-partum-psychosis/>

SP Energy Networks n.d., *Voltage Changes,* SP Energy Networks, viewed on 11 October 2019,

<https://www.spenergynetworks.co.uk/pages/voltage_changes.aspx>

Promises 2014, *What is the link,* Promises, viewed on 15 September 2019,

<https://www.promises.com/addiction-blog/link-between-empty-nest-and-depression/>

Wikipedia 2019, *Involuntary commitment,* Wikipedia, viewed on 15 September 2019,

<https://en.wikipedia.org/wiki/Involuntary_commitment>

WiseGEEK n.d., *What can cause an Abnormal ECG?,* WiseGEEK, viewed on 15 September 2019,

<https://www.wisegeek.com/what-can-cause-an-abnormal-eeg.htm>

Weatherspoon D 2016, *Understanding Why Blackouts Happen,* Healthline, viewed on 15 September 2019,

<https://www.healthline.com/health/what-causes-blackouts>

Wikipedia 2019, *Psychogenic non-epileptic seizure,* Wikipedia, viewed on 15 September 2019,

<https://en.wikipedia.org/wiki/Psychogenic_non-epileptic_seizure>

Wikipedia 2019, *Sphygmomanometer,* Wikipedia, viewed on 06 August 2019,

<https://en.wikipedia.org/wiki/Sphygmomanometer>

Wikipedia 2019, *Crimplene,* Wikipedia, viewed on 06 August 2019,

<https://en.wikipedia.org/wiki/Crimplene>

Ramji H n.d., *Wales 1970s,* Pintrest, viewed on 06 August 2019,

<https://www.pinterest.co.uk/pin/143552306848565491/?lp=true>

Telegraph & Argus 2014, *Savile 'groped women',* Telegraph & Argus, viewed on 06 August 2019,

<https://www.thetelegraphandargus.co.uk/news/11303926.savile-groped-women-at-high-royds-hospital-report-reveals/>

Wikipedia 2019, *Commodore 64 Games System,* Wikipedia, viewed on 04 July 2019,

<https://en.wikipedia.org/wiki/Commodore_64_Games_System>

WebMD n.d., *Valium,* WebMD, viewed on 03 July 2019,

<https://www.webmd.com/drugs/2/drug-11116/valium-oral/details>

County Asylums n.d., *Scalebor Park,* County Asylums, viewed on 01 September 2019,

<https://www.countyasylums.co.uk/scalebor-park-burley-in-wharfedale/>

Wikipedia 2019, *Chlorpromazine,* Wikipedia, viewed on 01 September 2019,

<https://en.wikipedia.org/wiki/Chlorpromazine#History>

Wikipedia 2019, *1940s,* Wikipedia, viewed on 01 September 2019,

<https://en.wikipedia.org/wiki/1940s>

Isbell T 2015, *Shell shock,* Haikudeck, viewed on 01 September 2019,

<https://www.haikudeck.com/the-mental-health-issues-and-hospital-treatments-of-soldiers-during-ww1-uncategorized-presentation-dymx8w26f3>

Wikipedia 2019, *Mirtazapine,* Wikipedia, viewed on 17 August 2019,

    <https://en.wikipedia.org/wiki/Mirtazapine>

The Workhouse n.d., *Bramley, West Yorkshire,* The Workhouse, viewed on 17 August 2019,

    <http://www.workhouses.org.uk/Bramley/>

NHS 2016, *The Mount,* NHS, viewed on 17 August 2019,

    <https://www.nhs.uk/Services/hospitals/Overview/DefaultView.aspx?id=3057>

Baker N 2019, *Silver Service,* eHow, viewed on 30 November 2019,

    <https://www.ehow.co.uk/facts_6748591_silver-service-waitress-job-description.html>

Chem Europe n.d., *Insulin Shock Therapy,* Chem Europe, viewed on 01 September 2019,

    <https://www.chemeurope.com/en/encyclopedia/insulin_shock_therapy.html>

Lomax J n.d., *Insulin Shock Therapy,* Britannica, viewed on 01 September 2019,

    <https://www.britannica.com/science/insulin-shock-therapy>

WiseGEEK n.d., *What is Insulin Shock Therapy?,* WiseGEEK, viewed on 01 September 2019,

    <https://www.wisegeek.com/what-is-insulin-shock-therapy.htm>

Wikipedia 2019, *Insulin Shock Therapy,* Wikipedia, viewed on 01 September 2019,

    <https://en.wikipedia.org/wiki/Insulin_shock_therapy>

Wikipedia 2019, *Amnesia,* Wikipedia, viewed on 01 September 2019,

<https://en.wikipedia.org/wiki/Amnesia>

NAMI n.d., *Schizoaffective Disorder,* NAMI, viewed on 01 September 2019,

<https://www.nami.org/Learn-More/Mental-Health-Conditions/Schizoaffective-Disorder>

Leodis n.d., *High Royds Hospital,* Leodis, viewed on 01 September 2019,

<www.leodis.net/display.aspx?resourceIdentifier=200947_168826>

Marissa K 2005, *Full Moon Crazy,* Psychology Today, viewed on 01 September 2019,

<https://www.psychologytoday.com/us/articles/200501/full-moon-crazy>

Poison.org n.d., *Activated Charcoal,* Poison.org, viewed on 03 February 2020,

<https://www.poison.org/articles/2015-mar/activated-charcoal>